GOD HAS A

Dream

FOR YOUR LIFE

Sheila Walsh

Published by

THOMAS NELSON

Since 1798

www.thomasnelson.com

God Has a Dream for Your Life

© 2006 Sheila Walsh

Published in Nashville, Tennessee, by Thomas Nelson, Inc.

Thomas Nelson, Inc. titles may be purchased in bulk for educational, business, fundraising, or sales promotional use. For information, please email SpecialMarkets@ThomasNelson.com.

Cover Design: Linda Bourdeaux
Interior Design: Mandi Cofer

Library of Congress Cataloging-in-Publication Data is available.

ISBN 13: 978-0-8499-0133-1
ISBN 10: 0-8499-0133-2

Contents

Contents

A Letter from Sheila

Dear Reader,

I sit here at my laptop in my kitchen and think about you. We have probably never met in person, but *something* made you pick up this book. It is to that *something* I write this note.

Several years ago, I picked up a book by Dr. Henry Cloud entitled *Changes That Heal*.[1] The only reason I was reading the book, or so I thought, was because Dr. Cloud would be my guest the next day on my television show, *Heart to Heart with Sheila Walsh*.

As I read, I took notes of questions that I believed my viewers would want to ask, but something else was going on inside me that was deeply disturbing. It seemed that God had given Dr. Cloud a clear view of my inner life. As I read about what it means to be able to bond to others, to be free to choose healthy relationships, and to "own" your life as an adult, I found myself weeping from a place deep inside me. I knew that I was not living in the freedom he described.

That was the beginning of the most incredible journey of my life. It took me from a television studio to the locked ward of a psychiatric hospital to the life I live today with my husband, Barry, and our son, Christian..

My journey has not been easy, but I wouldn't change a single moment. I used to live in a virtual prison. No one else could see the bars, but they were as real to me as a maximum-security prison. God saw those bars, and in his mercy he set me on a path to freedom. More than that, he gave me a heart to dream again and to believe that he has an amazing dream for my life.

My life today is not perfect, but it is *my* life. I still make good choices and bad choices. I fall down and I rise up, but I know I am loved and I am free. This is what I want for you. I want you to be free to love God out of a grateful heart, not out of shame or fear or obligation.

As you are right now, with everything you love about yourself and everything you would change, God thinks you are beautiful.

Perhaps it's time for you to trade in some old dreams for new or to reclaim a dream that has been buried under the frustrations and disappointments of life. And perhaps you need to discover or be reminded of the incredible dream God has for you.

God has given me a new song on this journey. It's more like a shout, really. I want to stand on top of a hill and cry, "God has a dream for your life!"

I welcome you to join in the celebration.

With love,
Sheila

Introduction

AUNT EM, DOROTHY, AND MRS. PIRIE

*[Dorothy] gave a cry of amazement and
looked about her, her eyes growing bigger and
bigger at the wonderful sights she saw.*

—THE WONDERFUL WIZARD OF OZ

*I'll give you a full life in the emptiest of places—firm muscles,
strong bones. You'll be like a well-watered garden, a gurgling
spring that never runs dry. You'll use the old rubble of past lives
to build anew, rebuild the foundations from out of your past.*

—ISAIAH 58:11–12 MSG

If you have never read L. Frank Baum's classic children's book *The Wonderful Wizard of Oz*, I highly recommend it. There is so much more to the story than the movie had time to tell. As a child, I loved the story so much. I have seen the movie over and over, but it is only in recent years that I have begun to see how much it has to say to us as women. The journey that Dorothy and her friends embark on has many parallels to our spiritual journey, so it is a perfect backdrop for this book.

Introduction

When the book opens, we are introduced to a very gray world. Aunt Em and Uncle Henry live in a gray, weather-beaten house in the midst of the Kansas prairies. When they look out their window, they survey a colorless and bleak horizon.

AUNT EM

Aunt Em has, over time, become gray. She hadn't always been that way. She had once been a pretty young woman full of dreams. But years of disappointment had removed the color from her cheeks and hair and the sparkle from her eyes.

Their home was a single, sparsely furnished room. In one corner was an old stove. In the center of the room was a trap door leading to a hole in the ground that served as a storm shelter. There was a table, three or four chairs, and two beds. The larger bed was for Uncle Henry and Aunt Em. The small bed was for a child. They had no children of their own, but in their latter years they took in a young orphan named Dorothy.

DOROTHY

Dorothy was not gray. The book doesn't tell us how she became an orphan, but despite her circumstances she still had the gift of laughter. When Aunt Em would hear Dorothy laugh, it so surprised her that she would scream and put her hand over her heart as if the noise was a health hazard!

Baum describes Aunt Em this way: "She was thin and gaunt

and never smiled, now."[1] The implication is clear. She used to laugh, but something or a series of somethings had extinguished her joy. Aunt Em no longer had time to laugh or to dream. When she looked at Dorothy, she wondered what this girl found to laugh about.

For Dorothy, that was an easy question to answer. His name was Toto. In the book, Toto was a little black dog with long, silky hair and small, black, twinkling eyes (not the Cairn terrier of the movie). He played all day, and he made Dorothy laugh. She loved him with her whole heart.

As the story opens, Uncle Henry is studying the sky, which appeared even more gray than usual. A seasoned storm survivor, he knew the danger signs. As the wind began to change direction and increase in speed, he called to Aunt Em and Dorothy to take shelter immediately.

Aunt Em's first thought was to protect herself, and she ran to the trap door. Her reaction surprises me; as a mother, my first instinct would be to protect my son, not myself. Aunt Em must have learned that there was no one out there to protect her or her dreams, so she had to take care of herself.

Aunt Em opened the trap door and climbed into the dark hole. But Dorothy, the true mother in the scenario, would not get in without her beloved Toto. The dog was so frightened by the noise of the approaching cyclone that he had crawled under the bed. As Dorothy struggled to grasp hold of Toto, the strangest thing happened.

The house was lifted by the wind and turned around and around three or four times in the air. Then it was carried for miles as if it were as light as a feather. Dorothy realized that the hole in the floor no longer led to the shelter but was now a gaping window to the earth far beneath her.

Once she regained her balance, she sat quite still on the floor for a while, being rocked by the storm like a baby in a cradle. It was dark and quiet in the middle of the cyclone, and Dorothy felt strangely at peace until she realized that she no longer knew where Toto was.

She looked around the room for her faithful companion and realized that he had fallen through the hole. At first, she thought that she had lost him—until she saw one ear sticking up through the opening. She crawled over to the opening and saw her little dog being bounced on the wind like a rubber ball. Dorothy grabbed Toto by his ear and pulled him back in the house. Holding him in her arms, she fell fast asleep.

Perhaps she dreamed of what she might find if she made it all the way over the rainbow. After all, Dorothy was a dreamer. Her dreams were not dictated by her circumstances but by her heart.

Dorothy is not the only dreamer I'd like you to meet, but we must travel halfway around the world to a very different place to find our next dreamer.

MRS. PIRIE

I looked out of the plane window as we began our descent into Seattle, Washington. I was fascinated by the sight of Mount Rainier covered in snow that sparkled as the sun began to set.

Just outside Seattle is the headquarters of World Vision, a Christian relief and development organization serving the world's poor. I was there for the next two days with some of my friends to attend a symposium about how we could become more effectively involved with their work.

I will confess that I was not excited about this trip. As part of a team of women called Women of Faith, I travel about thirty weekends every year and speak in arenas all across the county. The thought of one more four-hour plane trip was not appealing. I had no idea that God was about to give me a new dream that would change my life, my heart, and my vision.

During the next forty-eight hours, I heard many stories that left their mark on me, but the one I want to share with you here concerns Mrs. Pirie. Her story came to us by Bwalya Melu, who works with World Vision in Zambia.

Life is very harsh in Zambia. The life expectancy is about thirty years. The HIV virus and extreme poverty have orphaned almost three-quarters of a million children. Surely dreaming in such dire circumstances would be impossible—or so I thought.

During a trip into a small community devastated by disease and malnutrition, Bwalya interviewed a woman named Mrs. Pirie. Trying to discern the most pressing issues for a woman living in such squalor, he asked her if she could have anything in the world, what would it be?

I imagined that she might wish for a new home, clean water, or food in her pantry, but I was very wrong. Her reply was simple: "I would wish for a day when I could go into town and play with my friends."

Mrs. Pirie has not forgotten what it is like to dream. Unlike Aunt Em, whose perspective had become as gray as her surroundings, Mrs. Pirie still holds color in her heart. "The poor have a dream," Bwalya told us. "It is beyond clean water and food. It is to be human, to be free."

That night, as I lay in my hotel bed, I thought about Mrs. Pirie and prayed for her. Her vulnerability and honesty touched me deeply. I saw her not as a person in need but a woman with a dream, a woman like you or me. She is someone who remembers that freedom and the ability to dream are worth having above many other things. In fact, in some ways, Mrs. Pirie might be more in touch with her dreams than we are. Many of us live at such an intense pace that we leave little time for dreaming.

So what is the difference between dreamers like Dorothy and Mrs. Pirie and disillusioned women like Aunt Em? Why do some women, against all odds, still hold their dreams in their hearts while others allow them to be crushed beyond recognition?

What Happened to Your Dreams?

Take a moment to think about your own life. What did you dream of as a little girl? How have your dreams changed? Did you choose to lay them down, or did you have to? Do you even remember what they were?

What happened to your dreams?

I imagine if I could sit down with a woman like Aunt Em and ask her what her dreams are, she would probably say that she has no time for such nonsense. She might say that dreaming is just for silly girls whose only responsibility is to care for

*What happened
to your dreams?*

a nuisance of a dog. For Aunt Em, the four walls of her home had become a prison rather than a refuge. They were the reminders of what had *not* happened in her life. They were the constraints that made laughter an affront and dreaming a thing of the past.

I wonder how many of us in the church live that way too. It seems as if there is no time to dream these days. But if you study the Bible, you'll find that its pages are full of dreamers. There are stories of those whose dreams went unfulfilled. There are stories of those who exchanged their old dreams for new ones and those who received unexpected dreams from God that changed their lives and the course of human history.

There is also a promise of what will happen in what the prophet Joel describes as the last days: "I will pour out my Spirit on every kind of people: Your sons will prophesy, also your daughters. Your old men will dream, your young men will see visions" (Joel 2:28 MSG).

This text was quoted by the apostle Peter after the death and resurrection of Christ. On the day of pentecost, God's Spirit fell on the disciples, and they were filled with new vision and fire. People couldn't understand what had happened to these frightened men, so Peter addressed the crowd. "This is what the prophet Joel announced would happen: 'In the Last Days,' God says, 'I will pour out my Spirit on every kind of people: Your sons will prophesy, also your daughters; your young men will see visions, your old men dream dreams. When the time comes, I'll pour out my Spirit on those who serve me, men and women both, and they'll prophesy'" (Acts 2:16–18 MSG).

I believe that God wants to teach us how to dream again. I believe, too, that he wants to fulfill our dreams. It might not be in

> *It's time to dream again—and, knowing that with God nothing is impossible, dream big!*

the way we anticipate, but if we are open to his heart, this great adventure will change us.

It's a risky business to dream, for dreaming leaves us open to disappointment. But I think that when we stop dreaming, a part of us dies. So I say it's time to dream again—and, knowing that with God nothing is impossible, dream big! Perhaps like Dorothy and Toto, we might be in for the ride of our lives.

> *You did it: you changed wild lament into whirling dance;*
> *you ripped off my black mourning band and decked me with wildflowers. I'm*
> *about to burst with song; I can't keep quiet about you. God, my God, I can't*
> *thank you enough.*
>
> —Psalm 30:11–12 MSG

PART ONE

Follow the Yellow Brick Road

SET FREE TO DREAM BIG

1

Somewhere over the Rainbow

WHAT IS FREEDOM?

"Toto, I've got a feeling we're not in Kansas anymore."
—DOROTHY, *THE WIZARD OF OZ*

The Spirit of God, the Master, is on me because God anointed me.
He sent me to preach good news to the poor, heal the heartbroken,
announce freedom to all captives, pardon all prisoners.
—ISAIAH 61:1 MSG

*D*orothy was awakened by a jolt as the house was firmly set down on solid ground. It was no longer dark; sunlight was pouring through the windows. If you have seen the movie *The Wizard of Oz*, you likely remember that breathtaking scene when Dorothy opens the door and steps from her gray world into a world of vivid color. She was not in Kansas anymore. I know the feeling!

Our family moved from Nashville, Tennessee, to Frisco, Texas, in the summer of 2004. Tennessee is known for country music, Elvis Presley, and the beauty of the Great Smoky Mountains

National Park. Our old home was in the countryside just south of Nashville. My favorite thing to do was watch the sun set each evening. It would disappear like a fiery ball behind the rolling hills, which were a prelude to the mountains behind. In the fall, I would often drive up into the Smokies and watch as the leaves began their graceful turn from green to the spectacular reds, oranges, and golds of autumn. It was a breathtaking sight.

Now we are Texans, and we no longer have a fall. We don't have much of a winter either. We have hot, hotter, and "Help me, Lord Jesus!" It was immediately apparent to Barry, Christian, and myself that just as Dorothy and Toto were no longer in Kansas, we were no longer in Tennessee.

There are no hills where we live. The landscape is flat and stretches out as far as the eye can see, which makes the sky seem huge. I now understand why Texans do everything in a big way—there is a lot of space to fill. You need big hair and big cars to fill out the big landscape.

The popular country song certainly got it right:

The stars at night are big and bright,
Deep in the heart of Texas,
The prairie sky is wide and high,
Deep in the heart of Texas.[1]

I found this quite disconcerting at first. My homeland of Scotland is a country graced with rolling hills and spectacular mountains. As a young girl, one of my favorite things to do was to climb to the top of the Carrick Hills, which overlooked our small town, and gaze out across the ocean. I did a lot of thinking up there. God always seemed close as I looked out at the beauty spread like a fully laden tablecloth beneath me.

In my new home, I had a dilemma. Where was I supposed to do my thinking? I think God must have seen my angst, for suddenly one day I discovered Freedom Hill!

FREEDOM HILL

Our family calls it Freedom Hill. It's not very tall, but it is definitely a hill, and it seemed to just appear one morning. We live in a rapidly expanding neighborhood where it seems as if the builders frame a new house every other day. Cement trucks and earth-moving machines arrive every morning and begin attacking the land. When my dog, Belle, and I get back after our morning walk, I always feel as if I am chewing fresh dirt. In the evenings before supper, Barry and Christian join me on my little dog-walking jaunt.

It was Christian who discovered our hill. He suggested one evening that we should go left instead of our usual right turn at the bottom of our street. Always up for an adventure, we took off. As we passed unfamiliar homes and walked into a new area just prepared for building, we stopped and stared in wonder. There it was before our very eyes—a hill!

"How did that get there?" I asked.

"I have no idea," Barry replied.

With all the wonder of Dorothy as she opened her door and stepped into Munchkinland, we began to climb the gentle incline. As we reached the top, we actually had a bit of a view. The land had been cleared to build fifty new homes, but for the moment there was nothing there but one lovely tree. The builders decided to spare its life, and it stands tall, presumably also enjoying the view.

For the first time since we moved, we let Belle off her leash. Behind us lay a busy world of noise and traffic, but ahead lay a canine playground. She stood and looked at us for a moment as if to say, "You're kidding, right? Don't tease me!" But Christian took off at an athlete's pace, calling her name. Like a flash of pure white lightning, Belle was airborne. They ran and ran, while Christian cried to the wind, "Freedom!" It was a wonderful sight. Every now and then he would look back to see if we were still watching them, and Barry and I would cheer. We christened it that first evening—Freedom Hill!

There was something joyful and wild about watching those beloved six legs flying across freshly leveled ground. I see that picture in my mind's eye when I think about freedom.

THE TRUTH ABOUT FREEDOM

Although our circumstances may be confining, our spirits do not have to be confined. Internally, we can be free!

The ability to dream and to believe God's dream for our lives requires a liberty of soul and spirit. Although our circumstances may be confining, our spirits do not have to be confined. Internally, we can be free!

I wonder what comes to your mind when you reflect on the word *freedom*. Perhaps your first thoughts are of happy memories, going off to college, or driving your first car. You may think of external freedom, of someone released from prison or hostages liberated. As world events are piped into our homes every day, you may think of images from overseas. I will never forget the pictures of high school girls in Afghanistan who were able to take off their traditional burkas after the liberation of Kabul. Their smiling faces told a story of what it felt like to finally be free to expose their faces to the sunlight.

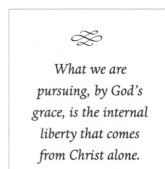

What we are pursuing, by God's grace, is the internal liberty that comes from Christ alone.

The freedom that we are looking at here, however, is not simply external freedom. What we are pursuing, by God's grace, is the internal liberty that comes from Christ alone.

"But wait," you may be saying to yourself. "Aren't all Christians free? Isn't that the message of the gospel?" After all, 2 Corinthians 5:17 tells us, "Now we look inside, and what we see is that anyone united with the Messiah gets a fresh start, is created new. The old life is gone; a new life burgeons! Look at it!" (MSG). Isn't this freedom, you say? The answer is yes. And no.

Let me explain what I mean by asking you a few questions:

- Do you ever feel trapped in your circumstances?
- When someone is unkind to you or treats you unfairly, are you unable at that moment to respond with the love of God?
- Is there any habit or behavior that you are unable to control?
- Are there times when fear completely controls your life?

- Do you still hear old messages from the past that fill you with shame?
- Is it hard to control your thoughts and bring them under the lordship of Christ?
- Do you still feel like a victim?
- Do you ever think that you will never get it right and that you have let God down one more time?
- Have you abandoned your dreams?
- Has your world changed from multicolor to gray?

If your answer to any of these questions is yes, then you are not free.

There are many things that hold us captive even as Christians. One of the greatest lessons that God has taught me over the last few years and continues to teach me day by day is that freedom is not the absence of bars but the presence of Christ. Freedom is not a changing of my circumstances but a changing of my heart.

> *Freedom is not the absence of bars but the presence of Christ.*

Have you ever thought, *If I could just get away from this situation or these people, then I would be free?* I remember very clearly thinking that. I perceived that the bondage, sadness, and depression I felt as a believer were because of external circumstances and people. But I was wrong. Eventually my circumstances changed and I was no longer associated with those people, but I felt exactly the same inside. The problem was not "out there"; the problem was inside me.

Through this book, I will share how God has set me free and

continues to set me free to experience the dream he has for my life. I know now that it is possible to be anywhere with anyone and, because of the power of the risen Christ, be free in your spirit. I promise you, this is possible!

What Does Freedom Look Like?

It is feasible to be physically confined but free as a bird. It is equally possible, and more common, to appear free as a bird but be in an internal dungeon.

For Dorothy, freedom existed somewhere out there—over the rainbow. She imagined that she could find a place where all the troubles of this world would be left behind. It would be a place where the sky is always blue and every single dream that you dare to dream really does come true. In this world, every trouble and care would melt like ice when the sun comes up.

Well, I don't know about you, but for me that concept of freedom has not worked. I am discovering, however, what freedom truly looks like—not over the rainbow but in relationship with Christ.

Let me give you a powerful example of what that radical freedom looks like from the life of the apostle Paul.

Maximum Security

In Acts 16, we read that Paul and his traveling companions were in Philippi on a mission trip. In each city and town they visited, they looked for the local congregation of those who loved and honored God. It was the purpose of their mission to tell as many as they could that Jesus was the Messiah and that he had risen from the dead. Not only that, but Paul was about to show those he encountered in Philippi what it looked like to be transformed by the internal freedom that only God can give.

Paul, Silas, Timothy, and Luke found a small group of women gathered by the river, and Paul began to teach them about the risen Christ. One of the women, Lydia, was deeply impacted by Paul's message and gave her life to Christ. She and her entire household were baptized, and then she invited Paul and his team to stay at her home. I love that God used a woman doing all she knew to honor God to birth the church in Philippi. What Lydia and the other new believers did not know was how God was about to honor their humble faith and demonstrate miracles through Paul's life.

The story moves on. A few days later, Paul and his friends were on their way to meet with Lydia and the new believers when a demon-possessed girl began to follow them. As she continually cried out that Paul was a servant of the Most High God, a crowd began to gather to see what was going on. This girl was a slave, and the men who owned her made money by using her to tell fortunes. The demons in her recognized Paul and would not be quiet.

After some time, the girl's cries became such a distraction that Paul turned to her and in the name of Jesus cast out the demons. This made her owners furious, for now she had lost all her fortune-telling powers, and therefore they had lost their ability to use her to make money. Her freedom would soon cost Paul his.

The men had Paul and Silas arrested on the grounds that they were inciting a religious riot in the city. It was against the law to disturb the Roman peace. What happened next was a multifaceted miracle!

After beating them black and blue, the soldiers threw Paul and Silas into prison and told the jail keeper to put them under heavy guard so there would be no chance of escape. He did just that—he threw them into a maximum-security cell and clamped leg irons on them.

A MIRACLE IN TWO PARTS

Before we look at what happened next, I want us to stop and take a good look at what was going on inside that prison cell. Paul and Silas were the only two arrested, perhaps because they were the group leaders or perhaps because they were the only full-blooded Jews in the group. Timothy and Luke were half Gentile, so in appearance and dress they would not have stood out in such an anti-Semitic climate and crowd.

Paul and Silas were stripped and severely beaten. I think it's easy sometimes to read the Bible as truth and history and forget what it must have been like. These were men just like your dad or your brother or your son. They were good men who loved God and had given their lives to telling people about Jesus, no matter what it cost them. Now they found themselves bloodied, bruised, and in severe pain in a maximum-security cell with nothing to take their pain away. So what did they do?

Imprisoned but Free

About midnight, Paul and Silas were praying and singing a robust hymn to God. They didn't ask God, "Why did you let this happen to us when we are serving you with everything we have?" They did what they would have done if they were at Lydia's house or in their own homes—they worshipped God. Their circumstances had changed drastically, but their hearts had not. Their bodies were in a physical cell, but their spirits were free.

We read that the other prisoners were listening to Paul and Silas, trying to figure out who these men were and why they were singing praise to God in such a dark place. Suddenly, at about midnight, the ground began to shake. It shook so violently that every cell door was thrown open and the shackles broke off the prisoners' legs.

The jailer, who had fallen asleep, woke up. When he saw that every cell was open, he assumed that all the prisoners had escaped. Realizing how much trouble he was in, he decided to take his own life. By Roman law if a jailer lost a prisoner, he must take his place and sentence. This poor man thought he had lost every one of his prisoners. Suddenly, Paul called out to him through the darkness, "We're all here!"

When the jailer saw that the prisoners were still in their cells, he fell at Paul's feet and asked, "Sirs, what do I need to do to be saved?"

God's Not Finished Yet

We are not told why Paul and Silas didn't leave when their chains fell off and the door opened. That would have seemed reasonable to me! It would even have gone in my newsletter as a miracle. I think that Paul knew by the Holy Spirit that the miracle wasn't over yet.

As it was midnight, it was dark, so the jailer had torches brought. When he saw that everyone was still there, he fell at Paul's and Silas's feet. He recognized that God was in this dungeon. That day, the jailer and his entire household gave their lives to Christ. Freedom would never mean the same to him again. He had witnessed with his own eyes what only God can do.

When God is present, anything is possible. I believe that for you too.

When we talk of God's dream for your life, I am not talking of the self-indulgent brand of spirituality that paints God as some kind of divine sugar daddy who exists to give us everything we want. That notion was very prevalent in the 1980s. People who taught this concept often associated it with faith. If we had enough faith, they said, all our dreams would come true—but they were very earthbound dreams, such as a bigger car or a nicer house or thinner thighs. To dream only of material or physical blessings is to settle for something unworthy of a daughter of the King of kings. I believe that God has a dream for us that will give us a bigger picture of who we are in him, not a revamped picture of the only things the world has to offer.

God is still in the business of liberating those who are bound. It is possible that you are reading this book in a physical prison. Perhaps a chaplain or prison visitor gave it to you, and you were intrigued by the title and picked it up. If so, I pray that God will

> *When God is present, anything is possible. I believe that for you too.*

show you that he sees you, he loves you, and he wants to set you free inside. It doesn't matter what has brought you to this place; God offers you a new beginning.

It is more likely that you are reading this book at home, and no matter how things appear to others, you are as imprisoned as a human soul can be. If your spirit is locked in a cold, dark prison, I want you to know that there is an earthquake coming!

God is still in the business of liberating those who are bound.

Some of the things I will write about in this book may seem controversial. They may shake what you have been taught as the truth. I believe that many Christians are in bondage because of what they have been taught by other Christians. We are called to be slaves to Christ, not to religion. As a culture, we are often more captivated by charisma than character. Jesus said to those who claimed to be his followers, "If you stick with this, living out what I tell you, you are my disciples for sure. Then you will experience for yourselves the truth, and the truth will free you" (John 8:31–32 MSG).

We can only be truly free if we understand that God knows all about us and loves us just as we are. One of my dearest friends in this world, author and speaker Ney Bailey, once said to me, "Imagine that a movie was made of your life. Nothing was left out. Everything that you have ever thought or said or done was displayed on the big screen for anyone to see. How would you feel?"

My initial response was that I would be ashamed. It is one thing to take refuge in the absence of what I might consider to be "huge" sins, but to have all my secret thoughts and feelings revealed would be terrifying. The truth is that we all hide part of who we can be when left to our own humanity. Then Ney said, "God has seen your movie, and he loves you anyway."

That truth is far greater than anything L. Frank Baum or Hollywood could ever conjure up. If we are to be free to experience the dream God has for our lives, let's stop here for a moment and let this truth sink deep into us, heart and soul.

The God of the universe, the one who holds the stars and the moon in place, knows everything about you

> ✦
>
> *The God of the universe, the one who holds the stars and the moon in place, knows everything about you and loves you with unprecedented abandon.*

and loves you with unprecedented abandon. He knows the good, the bad, and the ugly. He knows the things you are proud of and the things you hide. He knows it all, and he invites you to come just as you are and live the dream he has for you.

Somewhere over the rainbow doesn't hold a candle to this!

2

If I Only Had a Brain!

FREE TO BE THE REAL ME

*"I don't know anything. You see, I am stuffed so
I have no brains at all," he answered sadly.*

—THE SCARECROW, *THE WONDERFUL WIZARD OF OZ*

*He won't brush aside the bruised and the hurt and he won't
disregard the small and insignificant, but he'll steadily and firmly set
things right. He won't tire out and quit. He won't be stopped until
he's finished his work—to set things right on earth.*

—ISAIAH 42:3–4 MSG

One of the joys of living in Frisco, Texas, is that the entire Women of Faith team lives just a few miles away from one another. This makes it very easy when we all need to get together and plan for the following year's events or discuss upcoming writing projects.

Sometimes we meet in Luci Swindoll's house, as her library is so fabulous. It is built around a beautiful, long dining room table with plenty of room for all of us and our stuff! If our meeting time runs for more than a few hours and we need to include a meal, we gather at a small hotel that houses a more formal restaurant, a casual café, and private meeting rooms.

The memo that I received on what was to be my social gaffe of the year simply said that we would meet for lunch and then have two to three hours to discuss our theme for 2006. I spent the morning getting Christian to school, doing some laundry, and catching up on my e-mail. When I looked at the clock, I realized that I was going to be late if I didn't leave immediately. So I put on a fresh shirt and a clean pair of jeans and headed out the door. As I was a few minutes late, everyone else was already seated. The hostess told me that my party was in the formal dining room.

As I sat down, the waiter whispered something to Mary, and she announced that we were moving to the café. As we gathered our stuff and headed out the door, I asked Mary why we were changing restaurants. She replied that jeans were not allowed in this room. I was so embarrassed. Everyone else was wearing smart tailored pants or a skirt. I was the only one who looked as if she had parked her horse in the driveway. My fiercely loyal friends grumbled about the rules. The waiter was apologetic, but it really was my fault.

"I'm sorry, guys," I said. "I promise if we eat here again, I will not be underdressed." I am a woman of my word!

YOU SHALL GO TO THE BALL!

A few weeks later, we had another meeting scheduled in the same hotel, so I decided to have a little fun. I called Mary and said that I would intentionally be a few minutes late so that everyone would be seated when I arrived. Then I got to work.

It was hard getting into my car and even harder getting out. As I walked through the lobby of the hotel, all eyes turned to me. I just smiled, graciously. I made my way into the restaurant and stood at the doorway, waiting for my friends to see me. It was very busy that day, and soon everyone in the place had turned to see what was going on. When I heard Marilyn hoot with laughter, I made my way to the table. We had the same waiter that day, and he came over and shook my hand.

"This is a very good thing!" he said in his charming Italian accent. "You make us all laugh—this is good!"

When we are able to accept and embrace our humanity, we build bridges instead of walls.

I was wearing a full-length pink and gold ball gown and enough fake sparkly jewelry to land a 747. I looked ridiculous sitting with my friends in their normal attire, but I didn't care a bit.

Believe it or not, I don't like drawing attention to myself. I am not a big party person and would always choose dinner with a few friends over a large crowd. My point that day was to redeem an embarrassing moment and give us all an opportunity to laugh.

Laughter is so good for us. When we are able to accept and embrace our humanity, we build bridges instead of walls.

A RISKY ADVENTURE

One of the great adventures offered to us in this life is the gift of companionship and intimate relationship. It is also a gift that offers a plethora of potential potholes and landmines. We are all made differently, and accepting these differences seems to take a lifetime of work and grace if we ever get there at all.

When Dorothy and Toto stepped into Munchkinland, they crossed paths with three unusual characters who would join them on their journey to the great Oz. As their lives intersected, the first thing that was apparent to each one was where they differed. They might have stopped there and taken the potential relationship no further. Yet if they had done so, they would have missed so much. They would never have found what each one of them was dreaming for. This was a journey they were not equipped to make alone.

Although this is a story for children, it has much to say to us today as women. And it has volumes to say to those of us who love God and want to dream a bigger dream—the dream that God has for our lives.

Have you ever noticed that when you ask God for something, his answers are not always immediately recognizable? Dorothy was about to discover that too.

THE SCARECROW

She found him perched on top of a pole in a field. When, to her surprise, Dorothy realized that he could talk, she asked the Scarecrow if he would direct her to the Emerald City. He told her that he knew neither the Emerald City nor the mighty Oz. Dorothy was surprised at his ignorance. The Scarecrow explained that he knew nothing because he had no brains at all. Dorothy was immediately compassionate and offered to take him with her to see the great Oz. Perhaps he could give the Scarecrow a brain.

If I Only Had a Brain!

Where are all the Dorothys?

I wish there were more Dorothys in the church—those who receive us just the way we are and offer to come alongside us and help. One of the great risks in finding genuine friendships and community is being vulnerable to who we really are and who we are not.

I spent years trying to be what I perceived to be the perfect Christian woman. It is a miserable and lonely way to live. My great fear was that if I ever owned up to who I am and who I am not, I would be booted off the yellow brick road.

We all long to be known, but it terrifies us too. The great irony is that the foundation stone of the Christian faith is that we cannot save ourselves. We come to God through Christ, acknowledging that we have nothing of our own to offer. Then we live the rest of our lives trying to look as if we had nothing to be saved from! I have said it before, but I will say it again: we are not the good news; Jesus is.

Rather than judging the Scarecrow for his obvious deficiencies, Dorothy invited him to join her. She had no idea that later in their journey, the Scarecrow would save her life.

THE GRACE OF VULNERABILITY

What was it that opened the door for Dorothy's compassion? I think it was the vulnerability of the Scarecrow. When Dorothy asked him for directions, it would have been easy for the Scarecrow to say, "I forgot" or, "Don't bother me; I'm scaring birds!" But he didn't do that. From moment one of their encounter, he told

To be able to tell the truth means to have made peace with the truth.

Dorothy the truth. There is something very disarming about that kind of vulnerability.

To be able to tell the truth means to have made peace with the truth. It has taken me a long, long time to understand and practice this.

When I was growing up, I was acutely aware of what I was not: I was not the cute girl. I was not the athletic girl. I was not the girl all the boys talked about. I was not the girl all the other girls wanted to be like.

I meet women like this every weekend when I travel. Having lived behind the bars of feigned perfection for so many years, my passion is to see women liberated from this terrible place. It may look good on the outside, but life is miserable behind the bars.

How often do you look at other women and all you see is what they have that you don't? How often do you compare your gifts or personality or how your kids are turning out?

MYTHS DEBUNKED!

There is an unspoken myth among many Christians that the people God seems to be using are those who have been through tough times and are now victorious in every area of life. The inference is that this is why God is using them.

It means the world to me to be part of a myth-debunking ministry. The Women of Faith platform is not built on how good the speakers are but on how great God is. Our stories are not a list of things we did right but evidence of how God changed us in the midst of our brokenness.

Whenever I publicly address the fact that clinical depression is part of my journey and that I still take medication for it, I can see the look of surprise on many faces. More often than not, I see looks of relief, as if to say, "Do you mean that God still uses broken things?"

One lady told me that she knew I had been hospitalized in the past but assumed that I was now "fixed." I assured her that I was not fixed, just headed in the right direction—the one pointing to home.

TRAVELING COMPANIONS

When I was asked in 1996 if I would like to join the team of Women of Faith, my immediate response was that I would rather stick my hand in a blender! I had just turned forty and given birth to Christian. I could hardly make it across the kitchen, never mind an airport, and the thought of being a "women's speaker" was not appealing to me.

Let me explain. I have encountered women's groups before where, rather than encouragement to be real and free, there is pressure to conform to whatever the code is within that group. In life, one size does not fit all.

There is no one else in the whole wide world quite like you. When you hide or devalue your gifts and personality, we are all a little less whole.

God has made each of us with unique dreams and gifts. There is no one else in the whole wide world quite like you. When you hide or devalue your gifts and personality, we are all a little less whole.

Have you ever wondered how much pretending goes on in church? I think that the time we spend at church on Sunday mornings can be the least real hours of our week. I am not suggesting that every time Christian women are together we bemoan our sinfulness but rather that we bring our whole selves to the party. It really is okay to enjoy being ourselves.

Let me back up just a little here. Before we can *enjoy* being who God made us, we have to *accept* who we are. That in itself can be quite a journey.

WICKED!

As I write this book, one of the hottest shows on Broadway is the musical *Wicked*. It is the story of what occurred in Oz before Dorothy and Toto dropped in. The centerpiece of the story is the relationship between two girls. One is born with emerald-green skin. She is smart, fiery, and misunderstood. The other is beautiful, ambitious, and popular. These two unlikely friends end up as Elphaba, the Wicked Witch of the West, and Glinda, the Good Witch of the North.

I have to confess that I relate more to the Wicked Witch of the West than to Glinda. Glinda is everything I was not growing up. She is petite, blonde, and brimming with confidence. One of the funniest songs in the show is "Popular." In this song, Glinda laughs at the value some people place on brains or knowledge, for surely all that really matters is to be popular. She sings, "It's shrewd to be very, very popular like me!"

I don't think many women in the audience are tempted to shout amen.

ON THE RIGHT PATH

Between the extreme positions of Glinda the Good and Elphaba the Wicked, there is a path carved out for you and for me. It is a path cut out not by human hands but by the Lamb of God. It is a place where everything that is true about you meets everything that's true about God.

Isaiah 42:3 tells us that God "won't brush aside the bruised and the hurt and he won't disregard the small and insignificant" (MSG). Perhaps as you read this, you feel small and insignificant with nothing to offer. You may be bruised and wounded and think, *I've tried to be who I really am before, and it has left its mark on me. I'm not going to risk that again.*

DO NOT DIE BEFORE YOU ARE DEAD

During my visit with World Vision in Seattle, I met a remarkable young woman from Zambia. Her name is Princess. Princess has a radio talk show in Zambia to educate women on how to take care of themselves. The HIV pandemic in Africa is the greatest human holocaust to have occurred on this planet since the days of Noah. Into this darkness God is shining many lights, like Princess.

Princess's passionate love for God shines as she speaks about her people and her hope. I am usually an avid note taker, but I couldn't take my eyes off her when she was speaking. She has such a beauty and gentle power that I was captivated by every word.

It came as quite a shock when Princess told us that she carries the HIV virus. She assumes that is what took the lives of her parents, although they never talked about it with her. The only information her mother gave her was when she was in her midteens; her mom called to her to come sit on her bed one day. She told Princess to be prepared to take care of her brothers and sisters. In Princess's culture it would have been disrespectful to ask why, so she simply said that she would do that.

I asked Princess how her diagnosis affects her life and her work. She assured us that other than taking her medication, her life continues as normal. Then she said something that has impacted me to this day: "I do not want to die before I am dead."

We were all humbled by Princess's honesty. She didn't have to reveal her HIV status to us. She could have chosen to present herself as one who ministers to those who have been battered by this virus. Instead, she showed herself as one of the battered ones.

Do not let your dreams die while you still have breath in your body.

There was a palpable "moving in" of the group as she shared. It was as if we tightened the circle around Princess as she entrusted her story and her dreams to us. Statistics could dictate to Princess what the rest of her life might look like, but instead she chooses to live in God's dream for her life. She knows that even before she was in her mother's womb, God knew every step she would take and every day she would live. She doesn't wait to die; she chooses to live.

What a magnificent vision to live by. Not one of us knows how many days we have on this earth, but I will carry Princess's face and her words with me as long as I live. She refuses to give up and surrender to her diagnosis. I bring her words as a gift to you. Do not let your dreams die while you still have breath in your body. As Eleanor Roosevelt said, "The future belongs to those who believe in the beauty of their dreams."

It is never too late to be what you might have been!

3

If I Only Had a Heart!

FREE TO LOVE AND BE LOVED

"While I was in love I was the happiest man on earth."
—THE TIN WOODMAN, *THE WONDERFUL WIZARD OF OZ*

My beloved friends, let us continue to love each other since love comes from
God. Everyone who loves is born of God and experiences a relationship with
God. The person who refuses to love doesn't know the first thing about God,
because God is love—so you can't know him if you don't love.

1 JOHN 4:7–8 MSG

Our friends call us "The Velcro family." It is not meant as an insult or as a compliment. It is simply an observation. Let me explain.

We are a small family. There is my husband, Barry. He is seven years younger than I am and loves to remind me of this at regular intervals. I, in turn, remind him that women in general live seven years longer than men, so, all things being equal, we should pop off at about the same time. Barry is very handsome. The first time I saw him I held my breath, involuntarily, until a friend was kind enough to slap me on the back and make me cough. This was fortuitous, as there is nothing worse than meeting the man of your dreams and expiring all within the space of fifteen minutes. Barry is creative, is an expert in marketing, refuses to miss an episode of *American Idol,* and loves chips and salsa.

Then there is our son, Christian. When this book is published, he will be ten. He has his dad's face and hair but my eyes, smile, and slightly warped sense of humor. His favorite subjects at school are math and science. This remains a mystery to me, as there is no part of my brain that can grasp even the basics of math. He is smart, but he is also very funny and kind. He is good at sports, he loves to read, and he is a "wicked" skateboarder. Perhaps I should stop there. I do tend to go on about my boy.

Then there is Belle, our dog. She is a three-year-old bichon frise. I always know where Belle is. I just have to lower my eyes, and there she will be. If I'm working in my office, she sits on my feet. If I go into the kitchen to get some coffee, she follows me; and if I stop, she sits on my feet. When I wake up in the morning, I find that she has wrapped herself around my head like earmuffs. This was alarming to me at first. I woke up each day thinking that I had lost my hearing during the night until I realized it was just Belle. We also have a teddy bear hamster called Hamtaro, but he tends to march to the beat of his own drum . . . or wheel.

Barry, Christian, and Belle are different in many obvious ways, but they have one particular thing in common. They think it would be better if we could all somehow be surgically attached to one another. This drives me nuts!

Now, don't get me wrong, I adore my family, but I am also fairly fond of breathing. As a child, I suffered with claustrophobia. This was exacerbated by a night spent on a Scottish hillside in a one-woman tent that a sheep decided to sit on. The details are unimportant here, but the impact of being flattened by a large creature that refused to respond to shouts of, "Get off my face, you woolly beast!" has stayed with me for some time.

Two years after Barry and I married, at the grand age of forty, I became a mother for the first and only time. Thus, the Velcro family was born.

I know that as Christian gets older, he will become less attached to me. I see it already at ice-hockey games: "Mom, I'm sitting beside Dad. You make too many girl noises." I am not so hopeful, however, for Barry or Belle. So every now and then, I institute a new family rule: "I am going outside to read for thirty minutes. Do not come out unless the dog is on fire!"

Sometimes I run around in the yard, shouting, "Free at last, free at last! Thank God Almighty, I am free at last!" I can see Barry and Belle looking out the window. Belle looks confused, and Barry is looking at his watch.

I tease him a lot about this, but I am a very blessed woman who loves her husband and is in turn loved by him. Learning to love, however, has been a challenging journey for me.

LEARNING TO LOVE

I know that there are many Web sites available today that pair you up with someone who supposedly is compatible with you on many levels. I smile when I watch these commercials, for I'm pretty sure that a computer would never have put Barry and me together.

I love action movies; Barry likes comedy and romance. I like to read; Barry likes to talk. I think cell phones are the death plague of the twenty-first century; Barry takes his everywhere! Barry loves interior design; I just want a chair by the fire. I don't care if it's made out of leather or scotch tape, as long as it's comfortable.

Our relationships have the DNA to heal our wounds or to deepen them.

I have learned a lot in our years together. Barry and I have had a lot of fun, and we have also had some rocky moments exposing the woundedness in each other. It is in those moments that we have the greatest potential for change. I wish that reality was made clear to every starry-eyed young couple who float down the aisle together. More often than not, we each assume that the person we have fallen in love with will somehow "fix" us.

It seems to me that our relationships have the DNA to heal our wounds or to deepen them.

AFRAID OF MEN

I grew up with a fear of men. Because of my father's illness and the way an aneurysm affected his brain, his personality drastically changed. He quickly went from being my Prince Charming to being an unpredictable force. He never spoke again after his stroke, but he could communicate in other ways on which an intuitive child is equipped to pick up.

I knew when he was happy with me and when he was angry. The missing piece in the puzzle was that I had no idea what I was doing to evoke either of those responses. As a result, I became a very guarded child. After his death, I had recurring nightmares that he was coming to punish me for whatever it was that I had done to make him stop loving me.

I know now that I transferred this guardedness into my relationship with God. Through the cracked window of my soul, I viewed a distorted picture of love.

When I was eleven or twelve, I woke up one night needing to use the restroom. As I crept past my mom's bedroom door, I saw that her light was on. I was about to go in when I realized that she was crying. I had no memory of my mother ever crying. Something inside me told me not to go in, so I sat on the floor on the other side of the door and cried too. I decided that she must be crying because she missed my dad. That night I made a vow to myself that I would never love any man to that point that if he were gone, I would not be able to go on.

Because of my father's anger toward me as a child, the survivor inside me decided that it was better to be safe than sorry.

IF I ONLY HAD A HEART

The Tin Man, or the Tin Woodsman as he is called in the book, would disagree with me. The movie doesn't reveal why the Tin Woodsman doesn't have a heart, but the book does!

He used to have a heart. He fell in love with one of the Munchkin girls and determined to ask her to marry him. The girl lived with an old woman who did not want her to marry. She was lazy and used the girl as a virtual slave. Determined to thwart this impending marriage, she offered the Wicked Witch of the East two sheep and a cow if she would prevent the marriage. So the Witch cast a spell on the Tin Woodsman's ax. After a series of lesser injuries, one day his ax slipped and cut him in two, destroying his heart. The tinsmith could repair his body, but he could not repair his heart.

For many years I applied an anesthetic to my soul, only to discover that you cannot be selective about which parts of your life you deaden.

Dorothy and the Scarecrow listened carefully to the Tin Woodsman's sad story. The Scarecrow told him that he thought it would be far better to have a brain and no heart than to have a heart and no brain: "For a fool would not know what to do with a heart if he had one."[1]

The Tin Woodsman assured the Scarecrow that there is no joy without a heart. I know that to be true. For many years I applied an anesthetic to my soul, only to discover that you cannot be selective about which parts of your life you deaden. When you choose to contain pain, you contain joy too.

NOVOCAINE FOR THE SOUL

One of our favorite things to do as a family is to order pizza and watch *Mr. Bean*. Rowen Atkinson stars as the eccentric, hapless central character in this British comedy. One episode concerns his visit to the dentist. Unable to leave anything alone, Mr. Bean fiddles with all the instruments. The dentist looks appropriately put out at his behavior. With flailing hands, Mr. Bean attempts to explain and instead sticks the needle into the dentist's leg. Even though we have seen it a hundred times, Christian still roars with laughter as he watches the dentist try to walk with a numb leg.

This state of numbness may be funny to watch in a television comedy, but it is not funny in real life.

That is how I felt for many years. Even though I seemed to be involved in life and was cohost of a television talk show, part of my heart was numb. I don't think I even realized it, because I had become so used to it. Perhaps that is where you find yourself today, safe but a little cold. There is so much more for you than to be carefully kept. God wants to love you—*all* of you: the parts you show and the parts you hide. For that to happen, you have to be willing to trust. Easier said than done, I know.

God wants to love you—all of you: the parts you show and the parts you hide. For that to happen, you have to be willing to trust.

Pain is an intrusive teacher. It can drive us closer to God if we throw ourselves on his mercy, accepting that there is nothing we can do for ourselves.

Perhaps, like me, you learned as a child or as a young woman that it is too risky to trust, that relationships are best kept at a safe distance. It is not just in marriage that pain drives a wedge but in all relationships that threaten to walk on old wounds.

FREE TO LOVE

So what are we to do? Perhaps your story is far more severe than mine. I remember a very sad conversation I had with a young woman after a conference. She said to me, "You were lucky that your dad died. Mine lived." Then she disappeared into the crowd. I thought about her and prayed for her for a long time. What must her story have been to make that kind of statement?

As you are, right now, God loves you; and that will never change.

That's the trouble with love. It has the potential to exceed our dreams or to crush them. If you had a great relationship with your dad, then I imagine it would be much easier to believe in a God who loves you. Many of us did not have a good relationship with our fathers, so it takes time, grace, and the relentless love of God to win our wounded hearts. The love of God is the greatest news available to any man, woman, child, Scarecrow, or Tin Woodsman.

THE BEST NEWS OF ALL

If I had to give you my life's message in one sentence, it would be this: as you are, right now, God loves you; and that will never change. God loves you not because of who you are or what you have done but because of who he is.

Our behavior does not impact the heart and character of God. We think that on good days, God is proud of us; and in our not-soattractive moments, he loves us less. This is applying human logic to the heart of God, and it will always come up short. There is life-changing truth in the message of these three little words:

God loves you.

You!

Not just the woman who sits in front of you in church and sings like an angel.

Not just the woman whose kids learn their Bible verses while yours struggle to remember their names.

Not just the woman who has been happily married for many years while you are still waiting for a husband.

Not just the woman who is pregnant one more time while you weep with empty arms.

You, sweet sister. God is crazy about you.

When we grasp this truth, really get it as deep as the marrow in our bones, it changes everything. Now we have a place to build our dreams again. Now we are invited to set up home on a solid rock. Now we realize that there is no risk to abandoning ourselves to God's love. He is immovable.

There is a wonderful old hymn that we used to sing in Scotland called "The Love of God." I knew all the words when I was a young girl, but I didn't understand them. It wasn't until I was at my least lovable, by my estimation, that I finally began to understand that these glorious words are true:

I discovered that love and unforgiveness refuse to share space. One likes the drapes open; the other likes them closed. One of them will have to be evicted.

The love of God is greater far
Than tongue or pen can ever tell;
It goes beyond the highest star,
And reaches to the lowest hell;
The guilty pair, bowed down with care,
God gave His Son to win;
His erring child He reconciled,
And pardoned from his sin.

Could we with ink the ocean fill,
And were the skies of parchment made,
Were every stalk on earth a quill,
And every man a scribe by trade,
To write the love of God above,
Would drain the ocean dry.
Nor could the scroll contain the whole,
Though stretched from sky to sky.[2]

DROPPING OUR WEIGHTS

As I began my journey to the outstretched arms of God, however, I encountered a few bumps in the road. I discovered that love and unforgiveness refuse to share space. One likes the drapes open; the other likes them closed. One of them will have to be evicted.

4

Ding-Dong, the Witch Is Dead

FREE TO FORGIVE AND BE FORGIVEN

Oz had not kept the promise he made her,
but he had done his best so she forgave him.
—THE WONDERFUL WIZARD OF OZ

And when you assume the posture of prayer, remember that it's not all
asking. If you have anything against someone, forgive—only then will
your heavenly Father be inclined to also wipe your slate clean of sins.
—MARK 11:25 MSG

One of the many things that I love about my son is that I never have to wonder what kind of day he has had at school. It is telegraphed from a great distance. On good days, he runs up to my car as I sit listening to music on my iPod in the carpool lane, and he is lit up like a Christmas tree. On bad days, however, his dejected expression makes it clear that there is no point in going on with his life.

I remember one such day when he was in first grade. Timing is everything with Christian, and when he is nursing a fresh wound, he does not want to talk about it immediately. It is important for my expression to convey that I understand something terrible has happened and that I will wait until he is ready to talk. I am a fervent believer in the healing power of ice cream, so the local ice-cream parlor has become something of a personal pilgrimage—a veritable Lourdes for Christian and me.

So we sat there, Christian nose deep in a vat of chocolate ice cream and me with my microscopic cone of a fat-free, sugar-free, flavor-free concoction.

"I had a terrible day, Mom," he began.

"I am so sorry," I said. "What happened?"

"It's hard to talk about," he said.

"I understand, but just try," I encouraged.

"Well, do you know . . . ?" He named a girl in his class.

"Sure," I said. "The cute girl with the ponytail."

He looked at me very disapprovingly. "I don't think you will think she's cute after I tell you my story, Mom." Then he continued: "I had to share a table with her for art. We were sharing a big box of crayons, and she knocked the whole thing over on the floor. Some of them broke and the teacher was mad and she blamed me!" He said all of this in one breath, which only seemed to heighten the intensity of the crime.

"What did you say to the teacher?" I asked.

"I told her that she did it, but she said not to tattle!" Big tears began to form in his brown eyes.

"I am so sorry, sweet pea," I said. "Life is just not fair sometimes."

We drove home in companionable silence. That night, as we were getting ready for bed, I showed Christian Ephesians 4:26, which says, "Go ahead and be angry. You do well to be angry—

but don't use your anger as fuel for revenge. And don't stay angry. Don't go to bed angry" (MSG).

Christian's struggle wasn't just that the offending ponytail-wearer blamed him for the mishap but that she refused to apologize. I have great empathy for his position. Whether it's my Scottish genes or simply my sinful genes, I want to strangle someone when I feel that a huge injustice has gone unnoticed or misdirected. If you are going to offend me in word or deed, at least have the decency to collapse at my feet afterward in unabashed grief!

"Why would God ask me to forgive someone who is not sorry?" Christian asked me. That is a great question.

Why is forgiveness so important?

What does unforgiveness do to us and to our dreams?

How are we set free to forgive?

GOD'S GIFT TO US

My answer to Christian that night was to clarify the problem and then to help him understand and access God's gift to us in the midst of it.

I told him, "Life is not fair, and forgiveness is God's gift to us to help us live in a world that's not fair."

"What do you mean?" he asked.

"Well, if you don't forgive her and you carry this anger around in your heart, who does it hurt?"

"It hurts me," he said.

"That's right," I affirmed. Then I asked him, "Do you remember our flour walk?" He grinned.

Christian had experienced a similar moment in kindergarten, but this time the offender was a boy. When Christian told me that he had no desire to forgive the boy, I said that I understood and suggested we go for a walk. He was excited and wanted to take his skateboard. I asked him to leave it behind this time, as I had something I wanted him to carry for me. Ever the Southern gentleman, he agreed. When I produced a large bag of flour, he wanted to know why we were taking it with us. I told him that it was a surprise.

After we had walked for a few moments, he asked if he could put it down. I told him not yet. We walked a little farther, and again he asked. I said not yet. Finally he said, "Mom, I'm going to have to put it down; this thing is killing me!"

As we sat side by side on the grass, I told my sweet son that when we refuse to forgive, it's as if we are carrying a huge load around with us everywhere we go. Sometimes the person who has hurt us will ask for forgiveness and take the load from us. But what if the person doesn't?

We live in a world where not everyone is going to be sorry for the bad or thoughtless things they do. God saw that and gave us a way out. We can come to him and put the load down. God is always listening, always available. I told Christian that forgiving doesn't mean that what happened to him was all right or that he shouldn't be angry. It just means he doesn't have to be stuck with a ball of anger and no one going deep to receive it. (Please note this cool football analogy. Being Scottish and a woman, I should not even know that such a move is possible!)

The other truth that fell hard on the ears of this young sinner was Mark 11:25: "If you have anything against someone, forgive—only then will your heavenly Father be inclined to also wipe your slate clean of sins" (MSG).

I explained to my son, "If you want God to forgive you, Christian, you need to choose to forgive whether you feel like it or not."

"Good grief," he replied.

A WASTED LIFE

One of the most basic realities we must all face is that life on this planet does not work—at least not as it was supposed to. God in his grace gives us the tools that make it possible to grow even in the most unforgiving soil. But when we refuse to forgive, or don't know how to, the bitterness eats into our dreams and changes us. It puts our life on hold, as if to say, "I will not move on until this thing is fixed."

I once met a woman who was being held in that kind of prison. She waited until my book-signing line was almost through and then joined the end of the line.

> *When we refuse to forgive, or don't know how to, the bitterness eats into our dreams and changes us.*

"You talked about how important it is to forgive," she began. "That's easier said than done."

"I know that," I said. "It is one of the most difficult things in life to do."

"My husband and I were working together toward our dream," she continued. "He was going to become a doctor, and I was studying to be an RN. But four months before I graduated, he had an affair with one of the other student nurses."

"I am so sorry!" I said. "What did you do?"

"I didn't get to choose. He left me and married her," she replied, her jaws tight with emotion.

"Did you finish your course and graduate?" I asked.

"No, I needed time to get myself together," she said. "I never did finish."

"How long ago did this happen?" I asked.

"Twenty-four years ago." With that, she turned and left.

My heart ached for this woman who had allowed her husband's betrayal to cheat her of life. She lost not only her marriage but her career and her dreams. And she had carried that pain for more than two decades.

TRANSFORMED BY FORGIVENESS

To be able to experience the dream God has for your life, it is not enough to be able to forgive others; you have to forgive yourself too. Sometimes that can be more difficult.

I want you to take a little trip with me.

It's late at night and very dark. The moon is nowhere to be seen, and the stars seem to have vanished. The wind howls as if in mourning.

I sit with my back against a tree. I should go home, but how can I go home? How can I go on at all? I can't turn my mind off. Like a merciless abuser, it plays the same tape over and over and over: "Peter, before the cock crows twice, you will deny three times that you ever knew me."

I meant every word when I said that I would never leave him, but I had no idea that it would play out like this. I was ready in the garden to fight to the death, but Jesus made me put my sword away. Why did he do that? Why did he let himself be led away like a lamb to the slaughter? Why did I say that I never knew him?

It's all over now. For one moment in my life, I had a dream. I had a dream that I could be more than just a big, loud-mouthed fisherman. I

> *To be able to experience the dream God has for your life, it is not enough to be able to forgive others; you have to forgive yourself too. Sometimes that can be more difficult.*

actually thought my life mattered and that together we would do something big. Now he is dead, and all that mattered to me died with him. How will I ever face my friends again? They heard what he said, and they heard me say that it would never happen. I have nowhere left to go.

I can't imagine what the night of the crucifixion must have been like for Peter. He was the leader of the group and the one who had made the boldest assertions of allegiance. As he replayed the events of the previous twenty-four hours, it must have seemed as if rather than a dream, he was living through a nightmare.

Did he miss the amazing gift that Jesus gave him in that upper room? Didn't he hear what Jesus said, right before he told Peter that he would deny him? "Simon, Simon, behold, Satan has demanded permission to sift you like wheat; but I have prayed for you, that your faith may not fail; and you, *when once you have turned again,* strengthen your brothers" (Luke 22:31–32 NASB; emphasis added).

WHEN YOU HAVE TURNED AGAIN

This gift was given to Peter right before Jesus told him that he would make the biggest mistake of his life. He told Peter that he was going to blow it but that he would turn again—and when he did, he would dream a bigger dream. His new dream would have nothing to do with his own strength or abilities; it would be the dream given to everyone who has run out of his own strength and thrown himself on the mercy of God. It would be God's dream for his life. This is a dream worth dreaming!

On the third morning after Jesus's death, Peter was with the ten remaining disciples when Mary Magdalene and some of the other women who had gone to embalm the body of Christ burst into the room. They told the men that Jesus's body was gone. Most of the disciples sat numb and disbelieving, but not Peter. As if the wind was at his back, he tore out of the room and made his way to the tomb. When he looked inside, he saw that it was true. The body of Jesus was gone; only the strips of linen were left. Strangest of all, the piece that had been around Christ's head was neatly folded.

Peter knew what that meant. He had seen that before.

In those days, if you hired a carpenter to make a piece of furniture for you, he would work on it for as many days as it took. When he was done, he would take the cloth that he had used to put the final touches to it and fold it neatly. Then he would leave the folded cloth behind so that you would know that the project was finished.

What did Peter think when he saw that sign? Did he ask himself, "What is finished? Is the dream over? Is Christ's love for me or belief in me finished?"

The truth was that the work of redemption was finished. Only Jesus could pay the price for our sin so that we can stand in the presence of God.

Part of forgiving ourselves and moving on to dream big is accepting the truth about who we really are.

And for Peter, something else was finished: his passionate conviction that he was invincible and could never let Jesus down.

DO YOU LOVE ME?

It seems that part of forgiving ourselves and moving on to dream big is accepting the truth about who we really are. Peter wanted to think he could get it right by himself, but he couldn't. He needed Jesus. He needed to be forgiven and to forgive himself.

Just like Peter, I used to think that I could work harder and harder for God and that would be enough. I wanted my efforts to be enough to quiet the voices in my head that told me there must be something wrong with a little girl whose father turned on her.

For the woman who gave up on her dream to be an RN, I think she was refusing to forgive herself: *What's wrong with me that he chose another woman over me? Who do I think I'm fooling? I'm not enough . . .*

Perhaps you see yourself in her story. The circumstances may be different, but you believe as you survey the ruins of your dreams that if you had been different, your life would have played out differently. I would say to you as I said to this heartbroken woman, "We live on a broken planet where we are wounded and we wound others. Forgiveness is God's gift to us to live in such a place. Not one of us is enough, and that is why God sent Jesus."

Peter lived to discover that God's dream for our lives is far greater than our disappointing dreams could ever be. When it seems as if your life is over and all your dreams have died, don't miss the mystery of this place. Hide yourself under the shadow of his wings, and wait expectantly for the Dream Giver.

5

The Ruby Slippers

FREE TO RECEIVE THE DESIRES OF MY HEART

*"The Silver Shoes," said the Good Witch, "have wonderful
powers. . . . All you have to do is knock the heels together three times
and command the shoes to carry you wherever you wish to go."*
—THE WONDERFUL WIZARD OF OZ

*My whole being, praise the LORD; all my being, praise his holy name.
My whole being, praise the LORD and "do not forget all his kindnesses.
He forgives all my sins and heals all my diseases. He saves my life
from the grave and loads me with love and mercy. He satisfies me
with good things and makes me young again, like the eagle.*
—PSALM 103:1–5

As a little girl, I had a hamster called Rabbie. I purchased him
on January 25, which is the birthday of the famous Scottish poet
Robert Burns ("Rabbie" to locals). Just as Dorothy adored Toto, I
adored this little furry beast. I trained him to do all sorts of tricks.
I had a racetrack that I set up on the living room floor, and every
night Rabbie would go through his paces. He could climb over two
matchboxes and crawl through the cardboard tubing of three
empty toilet-paper rolls. As a child, I imagined that he loved this

nightly game. It now occurs to me that he might simply have been trying to escape.

When Christian asked if he could have a hamster, I was a pushover. Barry has never been around little animals, and they make him nervous, but he finally acquiesced when I promised he would never have to see it. Our new "family member" was crowned Hamtaro.

I gave little thought to how Belle might respond to the small, moving, furry creature until the first time Christian had Hamtaro in his lap. Belle came rushing over with her tail wagging and her mouth salivating.

"Look, Mom," Christian cried with delight. "I think Belle loves him!"

"I hate to burst your bubble, sweet pea," I said. "But you and I look at him and see Hamtaro. I think Belle looks at him and sees ham sandwich!"

I had a nagging suspicion that God might want me to do something with my life that I would hate.

As my contribution to peace in our time, I bought a little car at the pet store for Hamtaro. As he pedals along on the interior wheel, safely protected in a large plastic vehicle, he looks as if he is headed for California with great intentionality. Belle follows him everywhere he goes. In my mind, I see a cartoon bubble above her head that says, "One of these days that car will have to go in for repair, and I'll be right there!"

Watching the two interact reminds me of one of my favorite stories from childhood.

BRER RABBIT AND THE TAR-BABY

It was a story that I never tired of as a little girl. I think I loved it because it showed how even the most vulnerable among us can sometimes escape certain disaster if we are quick-witted enough. (No letters from would-be therapists, please!)

The main characters in the story are Brer Rabbit and Brer Fox. Not unlike Belle, Brer Fox viewed Brer Rabbit as an appetizer. Determined to catch him for supper, he set a trap. He designed a contraption that he called a Tar-Baby, put a hat on it, and placed it in the middle of the road. Brer Rabbit fell for it—or literally, he stuck to it. He was dinner for sure unless he could think his way out.

As Brer Fox mulled over the many ways to kill Brer Rabbit before barbecuing him, the rabbit's survival instincts kicked in: "'I don't care what you do with me, Brer Fox,' says he, 'Just so you don't fling me in that briar patch. Roast me, Brer Fox,' says he, 'But don't fling me in that briar patch.'"[1]

The fox threatened to hang him, drown him, or skin him, and each time Brer Rabbit appeared to welcome those deaths over the grizzly prospect of being thrown into the briar patch. Reverse psychology won the day, and Brer Fox threw the rabbit in the briar patch. The wily rabbit hopped off free once more. The rhythm of his bounce seemed to say, "You're bigger than me, you're badder than me, but I'm smarter than you!"

My personal version of the Tar-Baby story went like this: "Just don't make me marry David Cassidy!"

I tried that with God when I was about sixteen. I had a nagging suspicion that God might want me to do something with my life that I would hate, so I came up with my own little briar patch. I had a huge crush on the pop singer David Cassidy, so I told God I would be willing to do almost anything as long as he didn't make me marry David Cassidy. Unfortunately, the Lord seemed much more obliging than Brer Fox, and he took me at my word!

I Know I'll Hate It

I wonder how many of us have that mentality when it comes to God. We think that in order to make God happy, we will have to surrender our dreams.

I was quite sure that God would want me to be a missionary in some out-of-the-way region infested with large creeping, stinging creatures. The terrain would be so rough that I would have to wear flat, lace-up, sensible shoes for the rest of my life. I loved to sing, so I assumed that could not be what God wanted because I would enjoy it too much.

What a twisted view I had of my Father God! Perhaps it's one you share. Many of us are raised with very mixed signals about God's heart toward us.

The Desires of Your Heart

The psalmist David records this promise: "Take delight in the LORD, and he will give you the desires of your heart" (Psalm 37:4 RSV). Will God really give me the desires of my heart? This can be quite a confusing verse.

What if our desires are for things that are selfish?

What if our desires are for things that once gained, we wouldn't want?

What if our desires are for things that would harm us or someone else?

What if our desires are for someone else's husband?

Obviously, that is not God's intent in this passage. One of our human tendencies, which I think borders on heresy, is to take a verse out of context and use it to fit our personal dreams or fantasies. It's easy to skip over a few words to get to the bit that seems to offer what we are looking for.

The verse begins, "Take delight in the LORD." Only five words, but the weight of those five words could change your life. I don't say that lightly. I've been at too many Christian gatherings to throw out those kinds of promises with careless abandon. But to take delight in the Lord would change everything.

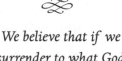

We believe that if we surrender to what God wants us to do, we will end up miserable on earth so that we can enjoy heaven.

Notice that the verse doesn't say, "Take delight in what God can do for you." It says to take delight *in him*. The very core of who we are as followers of Christ is self-denial. This is not an easy sell to people in our self-indulgent times. The irony is that within this call to self-denial is the most liberating truth.

We believe that if we surrender to what God wants us to do, we will end up miserable on earth so that we can enjoy heaven. I don't believe that for a moment. I believe that God has placed gifts and dreams in each of us to be a living demonstration of how creative and beautiful he is. But so often we settle for less.

When Bruce Wilkinson wrote *The Prayer of Jabez*, he had no way of knowing that it would become an international best-seller.[2] The book was based on one verse found in the Old Testament: "And Jabez called on the God of Israel saying, 'Oh, that You would bless me indeed, and enlarge my territory, that Your hand would be with me, and that You would keep me from evil, that I may not cause pain!' So God granted him what he requested" (1 Chronicles 4:10 NKJV).

Why did this book strike such a chord with so many people? What was it about this short prayer, expounded on by Bruce Wilkinson, that captured the hearts and minds of so many? It would seem unlikely for thousands of people to have been inspired by the life of Jabez.

All we know about Jabez is that he was a faithful man who loved God during a fairly uneventful time in the history of Israel. He asked God to bless him, and God answered that prayer.

It's helpful to remember that in the Old Testament, one of the marks of the favor of God was blessing and provision. "The LORD will send a blessing on your barns and on everything you put your hand to. The LORD your God will bless you in the land he is giving you" (Deuteronomy 28:8 NIV).

A New Way to Pray

When Jesus came and walked among us, God in human flesh, he taught us a new way to pray. In Christ, the focus of prayer shifted from God blessing us to us blessing God. That is clearly represented in Christ's teaching on a hillside one day.

The news of this man was spreading like wildfire. He taught like the rabbis, but he had a power and authority that no one else shared. Some people said that he was healing people, people who had been sick since birth! If ever there was a time for good news, this was it. Roman rule was crushing the spirits of God's people. Could it be true that God had finally heard the cries of his people and sent a deliverer? The crowds followed Jesus everywhere to hear him teach.

He didn't sound like a deliverer, though. His words would not cause you to dream great dreams of what could happen here on earth. He seemed to believe that to honor God and take care of today was enough. He taught that we should keep a clean slate with God and with others.

And he gave clear instructions about how we should pray: "So when you pray, you should pray like this: 'Our Father in heaven, may your name always be kept holy. May your kingdom come and what you want be done, here on earth as it is in heaven. Give us the food we need for each day. Forgive us for our sins, just as we have forgiven those who sinned against us. And do not cause us to be tempted, but save us from the Evil One'" (Matthew 6:9–15).

The elements included in this prayer of Christ are:

- praise for and confession of who God is;
- confident dependence on God's provision for each day;
- seeking forgiveness and forgiving those we have wounded;
- protection from the enemy of God.

Like Dorothy, my friend thought that all she had to do was tap her heels together three times and all her dreams would come true.

As *The Prayer of Jabez* began to increase in popularity, I started receiving many letters and e-mails from women who were confused. They had copied out the prayer and prayed it every day as instructed in the book, but nothing was changing in their lives. When I tried to glean what their expectations were, they ranged from new homes and new careers to new families and greater wealth.

One of my dearest friends had the prayer taped to the dashboard of her car, her refrigerator, and her nightstand. When her financial situation didn't change and no Prince Charming showed up on her expectantly lit porch, she was very sad and disillusioned. She has been a Christian for many years, but she didn't realize that what the prayer seemed to offer was the stuff of fairy tales. It was like a key to a treasure chest that had been buried deep in the pages of God's Word, waiting to be unearthed.

Like Dorothy, my friend thought that all she had to do was tap her heels together three times and all her dreams would come true.

I don't write any of this in criticism of Dr. Wilkinson. The trouble is not necessarily what he wrote but rather how we interpret it.

St. Paddy's Day Unwrapped

Every year on March 17 at 10:45 a.m., the Chicago River is turned an enchanting shade of green, in honor of the Patron Saint of

Ireland, St. Patrick. I wonder what Patrick would think of this annual "booze up" held in his honor!

As a young man, Patrick, too, assumed that to follow God would mean giving up his own dreams, and he had no intention of doing that. He was raised in a Christian home in Wales, in the United Kingdom. His father was a deacon in the church, but as he entered his teen years, Patrick wanted nothing to do with his father's faith. Around AD 400, when Patrick was sixteen years old, he was kidnapped from his village and placed on a slave ship bound for Ireland. He decided that this was the judgment of God for the way he had been living.

In his memoir, *The Confession*, Patrick writes about his years in slavery as a time when he came to know God intimately. As he walked the beautiful hills of Ireland, he learned how to talk to God and know him as a loving Father and companion. After six years, Patrick escaped and was able to board a ship home, where he began studying for the ministry. One night in a dream he saw a man holding a stack of letters begging him to come back to Ireland. He wondered how it would be possible to take the message of the love of God to the very people who had enslaved him.

He asked God what to do. In a dream he saw himself praying and asking God for guidance. From that day on, taking the love of God to Ireland became the only thing he had any heart to do. The Ireland of those days was a land of violence and death, torn apart by warring factions who worshipped a multitude of different gods. Patrick's passion was to let the Irish know that there is only one God and that he loved them. The tribal leaders and their Druid priests had a showdown with Patrick on his first Easter in Ireland as a free man. It was their tradition to light a fire on the hillside on that Easter Saturday night. There was to be no light burning but theirs.

In direct defiance of the pagan tradition, Patrick lit a fire to the Lord. As punishment, he was ordered to appear before the king of Ireland. He told the king that he was no threat because he came with good news about Jesus Christ, the Light of the World.

So what are we to make of this God-given promise that if we delight ourselves in him, he will give us the desires of our heart?

There are many legends that surround St. Patrick. But the truth is that this young boy stopped running from a God he thought would ruin his life, and he fell in love with a God who gave him a life worth living. Patrick had a dream that burned in him, heart and soul. He helped to drive out of Ireland superstition and dead religion. For twenty-nine years, he served God and the Irish people, baptizing more than 120,000 Irish men and women and planting three hundred churches.

THE DESIRES OF OUR HEART

So what are the desires of our heart that God delights to give us? Does God want to bully us into doing things we would hate simply to see how much we really love him? That doesn't seem consistent with a Father's heart. Many, like me, initially balk at what God might want us to do—only to find there is nothing else in this world that is more fulfilling and joy filled.

So what are we to make of this God-given promise that if we delight ourselves in him, he will give us the desires of our heart? I love what C. S. Lewis says in *Mere Christianity*: "Your real self will not come as long as we are looking for it. It will come when you are looking for Him."[3]

My own journey has taken me away from trying so hard to find the will of God for my life. It has taken me to a place of brokenness and letting go of everything I thought I needed. I found peace and purpose as I lay exhausted at the feet of the Lion of Judah. It took me many years to understand that God wanted my heart, not my schedule.

In his well-known prayer "The Breastplate," St. Patrick said it beautifully:

> Christ be with me, Christ within me,
> Christ behind me, Christ before me,
> Christ beside me, Christ to win me;
> Christ to comfort and restore me;
> Christ beneath me, Christ above me,
> Christ in quiet, Christ in danger,
> Christ in hearts of all that love me,
> Christ in mouth of friend and stranger.

6

She Slept Soundly Until Morning

FREE TO BE AT PEACE

*The Scarecrow . . . came near to cover Dorothy with dry
leaves when she lay down to sleep. These kept her very snug
and warm, and she slept soundly until morning.*
—*The Wonderful Wizard of Oz*

*Laugh with your happy friends when they're happy;
share tears when they're down. Get along with each other;
don't be stuck-up. Make friends with nobodies; don't be the
great somebody. Don't hit back; discover beauty in everyone.*
—Romans 12:15–17 msg

He had been watching her for some time, but she didn't appear to know he existed. He loved her smile, and it made his heart ache when she was sad. The wind would carry her voice to him at night, and he could hear her softly spoken words. He thought her quite beautiful.

He would leave her little gifts along the path he knew she took each day. She stopped and picked up every one, turning them over in her small hands before slipping them into her pocket. He left notes and watched her smile as she read them. They seemed to give her strength and courage, for afterward she walked with her head held high and her face to the wind.

He waited for her to notice him. He longed for her to turn around and see the love that was in his eyes. His dream was that she would choose to love him. As the months passed into years, he could wait no longer. One day as she began her daily walk, he stepped into her path.

At first she was surprised but then fell into step with him. For days they walked and talked, and soon it was as if they had known each other all their lives.

One warm summer night, he asked her if she would be his bride. She accepted the proposal with tears of joy running down her cheeks. She had no family of her own, but his family welcomed her with open arms.

At first she thought his family was kind and warm, but it soon became clear that she was not like them at all. Some of her new sisters were critical of how she dressed and the way she laughed. She didn't like that some of her brothers told her what to do and where she should sit at dinner.

She decided that she had been quiet long enough, so one evening she told her husband that she did not like his family at all. She no longer wanted to be in the same village and wished that she and her husband could go somewhere far away and never return. With great patience and love, he explained that this was her family now and it was part of her life to love them all. This seemed impossible.

She Slept Soundly Until Morning

AFTER THE HONEYMOON

This is an unsophisticated, rudimentary picture of what it is like to become a follower of Christ. When the honeymoon is over . . . you get to meet the rest of the family!

I remember the night I responded to the invitation to become part of the bride of Christ. It was a very emotional evening for me. As I listened to the evangelist, my heart was thumping in my chest. He said that God loved me unconditionally. He said that God wanted to have a personal relationship with *me*. I was quite a lonely little girl, and this was amazing news. Even though I had heard about the love of God since I was a child, it was as if that evening Jesus stepped into my path and met me face-to-face. I was overwhelmed.

I knew that my life would never be the same again, but what I didn't understand was how rough the path ahead would be. I naïvely thought now that I was part of the family of God—the inner circle, as it were—that we would love and support one another through thick or thin. There would be no more jealousy or anger, unkindness or separation. I believed that those of us who had accepted Christ's invitation to be part of his bride would love one another freely and gladly.

What had actually taken place, of course, was that one more sinner (me) had joined a large family of sinners. I personally found my sins much less offensive than other people's, but strangely enough, they seemed to feel the same way about their sins! For the next twenty-five years, I allowed my heart and my dreams to be shaped by how others responded to me. If I got great feedback on something, I made it part of my life. If I got negative feedback, I tried to minimize its importance to me.

Allowing the opinions of others to shape your heart is like living in a glass cage. It's pretty, but you are not free. Dreams die in glass cages. They need oxygen to breathe.

WELCOME TO THE BRIDE OF CHRIST!

Do you ever think it would be much easier to be a Christian if you were the only one? Then you could excuse the behavior of everyone else, understanding it is simply because they are all heathens! I say this partly tongue in cheek, but it's difficult to ignore the fact that Christians seem to find it very hard to get along as a family. It's not surprising, really, since we are all so different. We all have various personalities, character traits, and personal preferences, as well as spiritual gifts and denominational backgrounds.

> *It's difficult to ignore the fact that Christians seem to find it very hard to get along as a family.*

I will try not to get on a soapbox here, but I am making no promises. I place a lot of stock in kindness. We give great press to giftedness and ability, to being conscientious and showing up at every service and committee meeting, but kindness seems to have little curb appeal. Yet Jesus said, "All people will know that you are my followers if you love each other" (John 13:35). That has to be because loving one another is so hard—impossible, really—without the love of the Father, the power of the Holy Spirit, and the example of Christ.

Just as my son was indignant at the thought of having to forgive someone who did not appear to be sorry, we struggle to love those who don't appear very lovely or loving.

To Dream the Impossible Dream

Why would I include a chapter on loving one another and let it rest under the banner of being at peace? I am glad you asked! I think that very little disturbs our peace and crushes our dreams more than the area of our relationships. We are built for relationships. We thrive when they are good and healthy, but when they're permeated with conflict and pain, we suffer. We either strike out like a wounded animal or withdraw inside our shells.

One of my most difficult struggles as a Christian has been in this area. I am a fairly easygoing person. I don't get upset or take offense quickly. To have any hope of success at annoying me, you have to be really determined. But when someone does cross that line, I immediately pull away.

Let me tell you what the path to freedom looks like. On this path, we choose to love simply because we are loved by God.

It's my innate sense of self-preservation. Unfortunately, I have discovered that self-preservation is not a fruit of the Spirit! God

Whatever God has placed in you, use it.

wants us to live lives thrown open to his love and abandoned to his care. He calls us to love others with a generous heart.

When I look at the way Eugene Peterson interprets the famous love passage in Paul's first letter to the church in Corinth, the picture is staggeringly blunt:

Love never gives up.
Love cares more for others than for self.
Love doesn't want what it doesn't have.
Love doesn't strut,
Doesn't have a swelled head,
Doesn't force itself on others,
Isn't always "me first,"
Doesn't fly off the handle,
Doesn't keep score of the sins of others,
Doesn't revel when others grovel,
Takes pleasure in the flowering of truth,
Puts up with anything,
Trusts God always,
Always looks for the best,
Never looks back,
But keeps going to the end. (1 Corinthians 13:4–7 MSG)

How on earth is that possible? There is no earthly way to love like this. We are simply not wired to be that selfless. But I have discovered that in Christ there is another path offered to us. After being trapped for twenty-five years in a glass cage, I am now free. Let me tell you what the path to freedom looks like.

On this path, we choose to love simply because we are loved by God. We are not threatened, because God is in control. We are not defensive, because we have nothing to defend. We are not arrogant, for we are teachable. We are not bitter, because we forgive. We are not blown around by the whims of those surrounding us, because we have determined to hold on to what is true no matter what appears to be true. We are not easily offended, because we extend grace.

We choose to see beauty in absolutely everyone.

It's not an easy path, but I am convinced that this is the way to live. I have lived the other way for years, and it is miserable. When we live according to an eye-for-an-eye mentality, we are the victims of the emotional and spiritual well-being of others.

It's never a crime to make mistakes, but it is a tragedy never to try.

I dare you to live differently!

Don't turn your light down just because it seems to burn brighter than the one who stands bedside you. Let it shine and hold it high. The liberating truth is that none of this is about us anyway—it is all about God. If God has given you a voice to sing, then sing out for him. If God has given you the gift of mercy, then pour out that mercy in Jesus's name whether anyone gets it or not. If God has given you a heart to serve, then serve with your whole heart even if no one stops to say thank you. If God has given you the ability to teach, then teach with vision and passion.

Whatever God has placed in you, use it.

USE IT OR LOSE IT

Do you remember the parable of the man who, before he left for a trip, gave three of his servants money to invest? It's found in Matthew 25.

In this story, Jesus said that God's kingdom is "like a man going off on an extended trip. He called his servants together and delegated responsibilities. To one he gave five thousand dollars, to another two thousand, to a third one thousand, depending on their abilities. Then he left. Right off, the first servant went to work and doubled his master's investment. The second did the same. But the man with the single thousand dug a hole and carefully buried his master's money" (vv. 14–18 MSG).

What are the things that, when you are doing them, make you know that this is why you were put on this earth?

When the man returned from his trip, he wanted to know what each of his servants had done with the money. The man with five thousand dollars had doubled it, as had the man with two thousand dollars. But the man who had been given one thousand dollars said, "I was afraid I might disappoint you, so I found a good hiding place and secured your money. Here it is, safe and sound down to the last cent" (v. 25).

His master was furious. "That's a terrible way to live! It's criminal to live cautiously like that! If you knew I was after the best, why did you do less than the least?" (v. 26).

From this parable, we learn that it's never a crime to make mistakes, but it is a tragedy never to try.

We all have people in our lives who try to clip our wings. These are the ones who look at you as if to say, "Who do you think you are?" These people have for some reason let their dreams die, and it kills them to see the dreams of others flourish. But the truth is that whether you choose by God's grace to shine or hold back, you'll never make "Aunt Maude" happy. So I don't just dare you to dream big; I triple-dog dare you! Who knows? Aunt Maude might join you.

So what are your gifts? What do you love to do and really shine at? What are the things that, when you are doing them, you know that this is why you were put on this earth?

Once you identify the gifts that God has given you, don't be afraid to use them!

7

The Cowardly Lion

FREE TO LET GO OF SHAME

"You are nothing but a big coward."
"I know it," said the lion, hanging his head in shame.
—THE WONDERFUL WIZARD OF OZ

The teachers of the law and the Pharisees brought a woman who had been
caught in adultery. They forced her to stand before the people. They said to
Jesus, "Teacher, this woman was caught having sexual relations with a man
who is not her husband. The law of Moses commands that we stone to death
every woman who does this. What do you say we should do?"

—JOHN 8:3–5

*I*t is a sight I will never forget as long as I live. After the truck
drove away, I must have laughed for ten minutes. I had to get
Barry's approval to tell you this story, and the fact that he said yes
and laughed is a huge part of the story. Allow me to backtrack a
little first.

When I first laid eyes on Barry, I thought two things simultane-
ously: *Wow, he's gorgeous!* and *Good grief, how long does it take him to*
do his hair in the mornings? I had never met anyone more meticulous

about his appearance. He has very expensive taste in clothes, and as a single man, he indulged it freely. He has beautiful, thick, blond hair that seems to take forever to get just right. (One could read *War and Peace* and knit a sweater while he's getting ready in the mornings.) At the moment, his hair is cut in a sort of unruly, spiky, funky style with bits going this way and that. The thing that amazes me every morning is that he knows when it's "done." I mean, how would one know? It's like a living, breathing Picasso on his head!

As I got to know Barry, it became very clear that even though he's a perfectionist, he has a great heart and a great sense of humor. The more time we spent together, the more I loved him. I would tease him about his clothes and his designer-label snobbery. Once I bought a shirt at Goodwill, cut off the tag, and sewed on a fancy designer label. He didn't buy it for one moment! That's a true fashion expert. One has to admire that.

Don't Go There

I'll tell you in a moment why I laughed as Barry headed out on the truck on that beautiful March morning, but first let me tell you what brought us both to a place where the moment was so full of pure joy.

After we had been dating for a while, Barry decided to unleash his fashion "gift" on me. I was fixing dinner for us one evening in my apartment when Barry asked if he could look in my closet. I thought that a very strange request but acquiesced. If I had known what a floodgate I was opening, I'd have banned him for life.

He returned to the kitchen and announced, "You have no color in your wardrobe."

I said, "That's not true. Black and white are colors."

He dropped the subject for the moment, but I should have known better. A few days later, he appeared at my front door with a large package. I had no idea what it was; it wasn't my birthday or any special occasion. I opened the box, and inside was a new outfit—a skirt, a shirt, and a jacket. They were beautiful but nothing that I would have bought for myself.

"Why don't you go and try them on?" he suggested.

"I'll do it later, after you've gone," I said politely.

"No, please, I'd love to see you in them," he persisted.

Something deep inside of me began to close ranks. I felt myself pulling away from Barry as if he were attacking me. He could see it in my eyes and in my body language.

"Don't you like the clothes?" he asked.

"It's nothing to do with the clothes," I retorted with a definite edge to my voice.

"What's wrong then?" he asked, genuinely confused.

"I think it's very presumptuous to buy clothes for someone else. I mean, you don't even know what size I wear," I said.

"Yes, I do. I looked the other night when I was in your closet," he responded.

Well, now all bets were off. I didn't know why, but I was really angry, so I asked him to leave. After he had gone, I sat down on the kitchen floor and cried like a baby.

That night, I went for a long walk on the beach at the edge of the ocean where I was living in Southern California. I tried to understand why I had responded the way I did. Why did I feel so

> *When a prince buys an outfit for a princess, it always fits perfectly. And I knew deep in my core that I was no princess.*

threatened by Barry's gift? What was it about him wanting to see me wear that new outfit that sent me off the deep end?

The honest truth is that I felt a wave of shame come over me. What if I tried on the outfit and it was too small? What if the size on the labels he looked at in my closet was the size that I was *aiming for*? When a prince buys an outfit for a princess, it always fits perfectly. And I knew deep in my core that I was no princess.

A STREET PRINCESS

I remembered having a similar, though not as intense, feeling when I saw the movie *Pretty Woman*. Richard Gere plays the part of Edward, a wealthy, cutthroat businessman who stops to ask Julia Roberts's character, a prostitute named Vivian, for directions. Through a series of unlikely events, she ends up sharing his penthouse suite at a Beverly Hills hotel and accompanying him to various social functions.

Knowing that Vivian won't have the appropriate wardrobe, Edward gives her a significant amount of cash and tells her to go shopping on Rodeo Drive, the elite street of designer stores in Los Angeles. She sets off like a little girl on the way to a candy store, but her excitement quickly dissipates when she is completely ignored by the snobbish staff in an upscale boutique. They don't know that she has money and judge her solely by her appearance. My heart ached as I saw her sweet innocence and excitement replaced by shame as the store staff closed the door on her dream.

Vivian returns to the hotel with one dress from a different store. When Edward asks her why she didn't buy more, she tells him that people weren't nice to her. His response is very revealing: "Stores are never nice to people; they are nice to credit cards."[1] He, too, has been hardened by what he perceives to be the harsh realities of life. Somewhere along the way, he learned that the only thing that got him respect was money.

One night, Edward has tickets for the opera and buys Vivian a beautiful red evening gown to wear. As she takes it out of the box, her face lights up with joy. She tries on the dress, and it fits as if it had been tailored just for her. I was glad that the movie theater was dark—my eyes filled with tears. I was furious with myself for being upset at a dumb movie! After all, it was Julia Roberts, for goodness' sake. She's a movie star; of course the dress fits!

I was watching the movie with two girlfriends who were totally caught up in the romance of the moment. "Isn't she beautiful?" one whispered. "She is," I whispered back as I tried to unravel the knot in my stomach.

A DREAM REMEMBERED

There is a certain unmasked innocence in many of the scenes in this movie. The initial Vivian we are introduced to is a hardened street girl who won't give a stranger directions without financial reimbursement. Yet as the movie progresses, we are given glimpses of the little girl who had a very different dream for her life. I don't imagine that any little girl dreams of the day when men pay her in order to use her body and then walk away.

Toward the end of the movie, Vivian realizes that she is fooling herself if she thinks that someone like Edward would ever want her for anything other than an arm ornament, so she checks out of the fancy hotel. She can no longer deceive herself into believing that it is okay to be a call girl, because she remembers that she used to dream of more.

As a child, she would pretend to be a princess trapped in a tower by a wicked queen. She dreamed of the day when a knight on a white horse would come charging up the tower and rescue her.

How many little girls dream that dream? When life is painful and disappointing, we often dream of the one who will come and rescue us. We are scripted to think that way from childhood. After all, we were raised on *Cinderella*, *Snow White*, and *Sleeping Beauty*.

It's not surprising, then, that little girls dream of being rescued by handsome and brave men. For Vivian, life had taught her that no one was coming to save her from her mother or any other tyrant; she would have to save herself—or so she thought.

> *When life is painful and disappointing, we often dream of the one who will come and rescue us.*

The last scene is the stuff that dreams are made of. Vivian assumes that Edward is flying away on a plane until she hears a noise outside her window. It is Edward, with his head sticking out the sunroof of a limousine, waving a bunch of red roses in the air. He has come to rescue her.

The Cowardly Lion

OUR PRINCE DID COME

The outrageous truth of the gospel is that anything Hollywood or Walt Disney offers is only a shadow of what we are promised as God's daughters. After the movie is over, Vivian and Edward might make a good life for themselves, or they might find that

God's love for you is not based on your behavior; it is based on his heart.

when the initial romance fades they have nothing left. Cinderella and the rest of the Disney princesses received their first heart-stopping kiss and the promise of happily ever after, but then what?

As God's daughters, our Prince is not flawed or fickle. He has loved you from before you were born. He paid the ultimate price to buy you back and let his life blood seal the deal. There is nothing yesterday, today, or tomorrow that you can do to change his mind. God's love for you is not based on your behavior; it is based on his heart.

Life teaches us that if something sounds too good to be true, it probably is. Our Prince calls us to rise above the cheap lines of a broken planet and hear a better song.

A BETTER SONG TO SING

I remember being deeply moved by a line in the movie *Educating Rita*, starring Julie Walters. She is a working-class girl who wants more than her mundane life. Rita wants to dream again. She decides that education would be the path to her dreams and begins to tentatively pursue higher education.

Rita's husband thinks her new pursuit is pointless and burns her textbooks. Rita decides that she is fooling herself if she thinks she can carve out a life that has meaning or passion. Falling back into step with what has always been, she heads off to the pub on Saturday night to join in the singing of a drunken, familiar crowd. When she turns to say something to her mother, she realizes that her mother is crying. She asks why, and her mother responds, "There has to be a better song to sing."[2]

> *Shame is a dream killer.*
> *It's time to fight back!*

That one line sets Rita free, and she embarks on a course that will change her life forever.

As believers in Jesus Christ, we have a better song to sing. It is the song of the redeemed. So what keeps us from singing this song? For many of us, our songs are stifled because of our shame.

Shame is a dream killer. It's time to fight back!

SHAME EXPOSED

When Dorothy and her friends meet the Cowardly Lion, each of them needs something. Dorothy needs to get home, the Scarecrow needs a brain, and the Tin Woodsman needs a heart. It's not Dorothy's fault that she and Toto ended up in Oz. The Scarecrow had been made without a brain and the Tin Woodsman tricked out of his heart. But the Cowardly Lion has a different story. He is supposed to be brave, but he is not. That fact makes life unbearable for him.

When Dorothy and her friends first meet the Cowardly Lion, he has everyone fooled. All the other animals assume that he is brave, but that doesn't help him a bit. He tells the travelers that when he roars, everyone runs away. When Dorothy suggests that those who ran away must be even more cowardly than him, he agrees with her in principle, but it doesn't bring him any relief. He knows at his core that he is a coward and hates himself because of it.

As I read that part of the story again, it pierced my heart, because I feel a great affinity with the Cowardly Lion. I wonder if you do too.

When we feel shame at our core, it doesn't matter if everyone else thinks that we are fine. We still feel like a used-car salesman, not sure that what we sold you will get you all the way home.

> *When we feel shame at our core, it doesn't matter if everyone else thinks that we are fine. We still feel like a used-car salesman, not sure that what we sold you will get you all the way home.*

Shame is when we despise who we are as opposed to what we do. That makes it a very insidious disease. If we have done something wrong, we can try and put it right. But if we believe that we *are* something wrong, then what can we do?

We are lost unless someone sees the whole truth about us and loves and receives us anyway. We are saved if that someone is the Son of God.

RECOGNIZED AND REDEEMED

I wonder what it felt like to be the woman in John's Gospel who had been caught in the act of adultery. Her face burning with shame, she was hauled in front of a crowd of so-called respectable people and exposed as a sinner. She had no defense. She had been caught in the act, and now her life was over. They made her stand there as they discussed her fate with this man.

Why were they letting this Jewish teacher decide what should happen to her? Who was this man? Her shame circled her like fire, separating her from decent people until he spoke. He gave out rock-throwing privileges to the first man among them who had never sinned. She was confused. There was a difference between the kind of sin that she committed and the kind that respectable people committed. Everyone knew that, didn't they?

He waited. She waited, her heart pounding like a hammer on wood, like a stone on flesh. One by one, they all walked away. He looked her in the eyes and asked if there was no one left to condemn her. She admitted that there was no one left, because they had all disappeared like bats in the daylight.

His next sentence changed her forever: "I also don't judge you guilty. You may go now, but don't sin anymore" (John 8:11).

He knew who she was and what she had done, and he didn't judge her. Not only that; he gave her the chance to dream again.

"Don't do that anymore."

"Choose a different life."

"Be a different woman."

"Dream a bigger dream."

He talked as someone who knew what he was talking about,

and he was giving her dreams another chance.

That is the hope for every one of us. The cross of Calvary is a place to drop our overcoats of shame. It is the place where all that is true about us and all that is false meet the grace and mercy of God.

> *Have your dreams been crushed by a sense that you don't belong or you will never measure up?*

I have been to that place and dropped the coat of shame. My sweet husband has been there too. We have both experienced what it is like to be exposed for who we really are and loved at the same time. It is breathtaking!

Will you take a moment and consider your life?

Are there roots of shame interwoven with who you really are?

Have your dreams been crushed by a sense that you don't belong or you will never measure up?

Is it possible for you to believe that God knows everything about you and loves and accepts you too?

RHINESTONE COWBOY

As I watched Barry drive off that morning, I laughed with the unbridled joy of one who understands that we are all a little bit "off," but we are also loved.

I had been invited to speak at a banquet in the Texas hill country. Our accommodations were at a hunting reserve. When I told Barry and Christian that they had been invited to go hunting, Christian was over the moon about the idea. To his credit, Barry agreed to come to support his son. He came down to breakfast the first morning in his expensive, Italian-designed Prada leather jacket and boots. Our host, Philip, took one look at him and said, "You might want to consider another outfit."

This was all that Barry had, so Philip kitted him out in a camouflage jacket, work boots, and a cowboy hat. As I watched my husband drive off on the back of a beat-up pickup truck with a big grin on his face, I thought to myself, *Lord, everyone should be so free.*

As the dust began to settle after the pickup truck had left, I sat on the deck of the ranch house and thought about how far God had brought me from cowering in the closet to standing in the sunshine.

No matter how things seem, God is in control, and we are his daughters.

Shame is a loud and ravenous companion. No matter how much you feed it, it always wants more. I could spend more money than I do on new clothes and makeup, but underneath it all I would still hear the same growl of discontent. Shame put a cap on my dreams. It told me which ones were possible and which ones were not. It always wrapped its lies in semitruth so they seemed reasonable:

You live on a broken planet, so of course you remain broken.
You will have to deal with your shabby self down here until you receive your new self in heaven.
How can you expect to feel like a princess down here when it is clear that chaos is in control?

I no longer accept these things to be true. We do live on a broken planet, but we have been rescued. When God looks at us, he says that we are beautiful, fearfully and wonderfully made. And no matter how things seem, God is in control, and we are his daughters.

I think it is time to start living like it!

8

Glinda the Good

FREE TO BE A PRINCESS

Dorothy's first act was to call all the Winkies together
and tell them they were no longer slaves.
—THE WONDERFUL WIZARD OF OZ

I was in trouble, so I called to the LORD. *The* LORD *answered*
me and set me free. I will not be afraid, because the LORD *is with*
me. People can't do anything to me. The LORD *is with me to help me,*
so I will see my enemies defeated. It is better to trust the LORD *than*
to trust people. It is better to trust the LORD *than to trust princes.*
—PSALM 118:5–9

I was excited and nervous as I opened the box. It was a huge leap of faith for me to be this vulnerable to anyone, but Barry had shown me in so many ways that I could trust him. I looked inside expecting to see my Catwoman costume, but what was staring back at me was nothing like the sleek Catwoman costume I expected. I didn't know whether to laugh or cry, but having spent many moments of my life in tears over how I looked, I decided it was time to laugh.

Let me back up a little here and explain my furry surprise.

A Princess or a Superhero?

When I was a little girl, my girlfriends and I fell into two separate camps: those who saw themselves as princesses and those who saw themselves as superheroes.

Princesses loved to wear dresses and put ribbons in their hair. They were usually petite and dainty and knew that they were princesses because their daddies told them so. Superheroes, also known as tomboys, liked to climb trees and could ride their bikes without holding on to the handlebars. They were usually covered in bruises from past rescue missions. They had little use for ribbons unless it was to make a leash for their pet hamster, like my Sir Rabbie the Bold.

On reflection, I don't think tomboys or superheroes were ever told by their daddies that they could be princesses. Perhaps like me, their dad had died, or maybe he had just never thought to tell them. It's possible that no one ever told him he was a prince.

Princesses seemed vulnerable to me. They looked as if they were always in need of someone to rescue them. I didn't want to need rescuing; I wanted to *be* the rescuer. I wanted to be a superhero so I could take care of myself and others. As far as I could tell, girls who were princesses were likely to be rescued because they were beautiful and very thin. I was neither. I didn't want to be that needy, so I created around me a myth of strength and independence.

One day as I was flicking through the three channels offered to us at that time in Scotland, I found a perfect role model.

Glinda the Good

Wonder Woman

In the original Marvel comic book, Wonder Woman was described by her creator, William Moulton Marston, as "beautiful as Aphrodite, wise as Athena, stronger than Hercules and swifter than Mercury." If you skipped over the Aphrodite bit, she was my kind of woman.

I liked almost everything about her. I loved the cape and boots and the gold headband . . . I just struggled with the body suit. In my opinion, Scottish women cannot or should not wear spandex. For a start, we are too white. The sun doesn't shine much in Scotland, so there is very little sunbathing time. That much white flesh should never be exposed in spandex.

Second, Scottish women tend to be short. I look fairly tall on stage, but when I take my shoes off, I am well on my way to becoming a garden gnome! All the women in my family end up with osteoporosis, so we shrink as we age. If any of us live too long, we will just fold up and collapse.

I think it is clear that it would be hard for a short, pale person to pull off Wonder Woman's red, white, and blue leotard. All that aside, she was still my hero, and I made peace with the discrepancies by reasoning that if she lived in Scotland, she would wear more clothes and be a little less Amazonian.

I have talked a little about the shame issues that haunted me for years. It was that sense of self-loathing that made me shy away from any idea of being a princess or a damsel in distress. Even as I write these words, it grieves me to think of any daughter of the King of kings feeling as I did, but I include them because I know that many still do.

On my wedding day, I would receive an unlikely gift that would show me how far God had brought me.

THE WEDDING

Many women have told me that their wedding day was wonderful but the first year of marriage was difficult. My experience is the opposite. Our first year of marriage was wonderful, but our wedding day was laced with disaster. It actually started long before the ceremony.

One of my bridesmaids was my dear friend Marlene Rice. (I intended to omit her part of this tale, but when I told her that I was writing about the wedding, she told me I should absolutely include it. What a woman!)

When it was time to order the bridesmaids' dresses, I asked Marlene what size she wanted me to order. I told her that the girl in the store had advised that we all go up one size, as formal dresses tend to run small. She said that I should order a size 12.

I was a bit doubtful that a 12 would fit, so I suggested we order a 14, to give her room to breathe and eat. She said that a 12 would be just fine. (Marlene has been on a diet for thirty-five years. It wasn't working yet, but she believed it could kick in at any moment.) I didn't want to hurt her feelings, so I ordered a 14 and cut off the label before I took it over to her house. She pulled it out of the box and asked, "Did you order a 14 and cut the label off?"

"Yes, I did," I admitted. "Why don't you try it on?"

Marlene disappeared into the bedroom, muttering something

that I think was from the Psalms. She came out a few moments later, pale and quiet. "I can't get the zipper up!"

We stared at each other for a moment and then burst out laughing.

"What will we do?" I asked. "I know, I'll see if I can get a 16 in time."

"No way!" she said. "I'll go on a diet."

"But you only have three weeks," I reminded her.

"I can do it. I have to do it!" was her determined response.

With only five days to go, things were not looking good, and Marlene was desperate. Searching through the phone book, looking for anyone who might offer a miracle, she came across a store called Inches Off. Although it was in a very seedy part of town, Marlene decided to brave it. The advertisement promised the loss of inches in a matter of hours.

She recalls, "It was located next to an adult video store, and the windows weren't tinted, so everyone walking into the store looked in at us first. They would laugh hysterically as they watched us— dressed in our blue plastic suits, sweating profusely as the exercise machines rotated our bodies around. The machines had to do for us what we couldn't do for ourselves, because under those suits were the "Pillsbury Dough Girls." We were double-wrapped in mud from the Dead Sea—as in Israel. It was an experience of biblical proportions!

Five days later, Marlene could zip up the dress. She couldn't sit down but she could at least stand up, which was more than could be said for one of Barry's groomsmen. At the rehearsal in the church on the evening before the wedding I noticed that "Bill" kept falling over. I asked Barry what was wrong, and he told me that his friend had a genetic disorder and couldn't stand up for more than fifteen minutes.

"Did that not seem relevant to you when you asked him to be a groomsman?" I asked.

"I forgot!" he said.

"Not a problem," I replied. "We'll prop him up beside one of the pillars at the altar."

Somehow I got through the service. It was hard to look to my right or my left. To my right was Marlene, who was fast turning purple, and to my left was "Bill," leaning against a pillar, sweating profusely.

Finally Barry and I were man and wife. As we sat in our horse-drawn carriage, heading for the reception, I asked Barry about something that had been bothering me all day. "Babe, your dad sent a limo to pick me up at the hotel and take me to the church."

"I know. Wasn't that nice?" he said.

"It was fabulous," I agreed. "But everyone bowed their heads as we passed by. That seemed strange. Why was that?"

Barry grinned. "Dad got a deal," he said.

"What do you mean, a deal?" I asked.

"He knows the guy who owns the funeral parlor, so he got a good deal on it. It's a funeral limo. It's taking us to our hotel tonight too!"

We laughed all the way to the reception, which was a good thing, considering that when we arrived, we discovered that the caterer had made a huge mistake and all the food was gone in five minutes.

Then, as we were getting ready to leave the reception, I saw smoke coming from the kitchen. The chef apologized for incinerating the supper that is traditionally sent with the bride and groom in Charleston, but to me it just added to the black comedy of the day.

I changed into my going-away suit, and the photographer and all our friends and family gathered downstairs to wave us off. There was no limousine in sight. It was only later that we discovered someone had died and they needed it! I would love to say that I am exaggerating, but actually there is more that I will spare you from.

MY FINAL MISSION

I had planned a little surprise for Barry at our hotel. It was clear to both of us as we became closer that I had a strong instinct toward self-preservation. We joked about my superhero image, but he understood that there was a lot of pain under the cloak. I didn't want to live like Aunt Em, safe and gray. I wanted to be like Dorothy and still dream in color. So I decided that on my wedding night, I would surrender my superhero cloak and boots for good.

I wanted to be creative, so I did some research on superhero costumes. I intended to order Wonder Woman but it was out of stock, so I settled for Catwoman instead. The picture showed a sleek, black, shiny costume. I planned to put it on, leap out of the bathroom, and announce that I was retiring and this would be my last mission: to rescue Barry from the cold and cruel world of bachelorhood. (How corny is that!)

I told Barry that I had a surprise and took the box into the bath-room. I'm sure he wondered what on earth a good Baptist girl was going to produce from the box! I opened the box and looked inside. I looked again. I began rummaging through the box, thinking that the right costume must be hiding. Then I realized what had happened. I couldn't believe it: they had sent me the wrong costume altogether.

I decided to put it on anyway. I will never forget Barry's expression as he looked at his new bride. Instead of sending me Catwoman, they had sent me a big, fat, hairy cat suit! It was a man-size, furry, orange, tabby-cat suit. I looked like Garfield. Hardly the stuff any man dreams of on his wedding night!

In that moment when everything went wrong, I saw how God had put things right in my heart and soul. Only God could have helped me see how funny it was to come out of the bathroom on my honeymoon night looking like the Cowardly Lion instead of Michelle Pfeiffer. The truth is that I felt beautiful! Even though I looked like an alley cat, I felt like a princess. I know now that in God's eyes I had been a true princess all along, but I just didn't know it.

> *In that moment when everything went wrong, I saw how God had put things right in my heart and soul.*

DISCOVERING WHO YOU REALLY ARE

In the book, Dorothy and her friends don't meet Glinda, the Good Witch of the North, until the very end of their journey. When they are granted an audience in her palace, Glinda's first task is to make sure that the Scarecrow, the Tin Woodsman, and the Cowardly

Lion all make it back to their new homes. Dorothy is touched by her kindness but says, "You have not yet told me how to get back to Kansas."

Glinda tells Dorothy that her shoes have the power to take her back. If she had understood their power, she could have gone home on the very first day. But she didn't know what she had been given or, consequently, who she was.

> *Once you know who you are, you can never be fooled again.*

Perhaps that is part of the adventure offered to us, too, as God's daughters—the journey to find out who we really are. Once you know who you are, you can never be fooled again.

BITTER NO MORE

The Bible is full of stories of women who had no idea who they really were until they came face-to-face with God, and the truth of that encounter became a transforming moment.

Think of Ruth and Naomi. Israel was experiencing extreme famine, so Elimelech, his wife, and their two sons came to Moab to find food. They not only found food but both sons found wives among the Moabite women. Then, Elimelech died. His wife, Naomi, and their children lived in Moab for ten more years; then tragedy struck. We are not told how it happened, but both sons died. (Their names, Mahlon and Kilion, mean "sickly" and "failing" in Hebrew, so that may be a bit of a clue right there!)

Neither son had any children, so Naomi told her Moabite daughters-in-law, Ruth and Orpah, to go back to their families and try to begin new lives. Orpah agreed and went home to her family, but Ruth refused to leave Naomi alone. I love her poetic gift to her mother-in-law:

> Entreat me not to leave you,
> Or to turn back from following after you;
> For wherever you go, I will go;
> And wherever you lodge, I will lodge;
> Your people shall be my people,
> And your God, my God.
> Where you die, I will die,
> And there will I be buried.
> The LORD do so to me, and more also,
> If anything but death parts you and me. (Ruth 1:16–18 NKJV)

Ruth had no way of knowing that when she refused to leave her mother-in-law and returned instead with her to Israel, she had slipped her life under the wings of the almighty God. Everything was about to change for these two women.

DAUGHTERS OF THE KING

Naomi was convinced that her life was over. She returned with Ruth to her hometown of Bethlehem. Her old friends were thrilled to see her, but she asked them to no longer call her Naomi, which means pleasant or lovely, but to call her Mara, which means bitter. She had left her homeland full of life and blessing and was returning, as far as she could see, empty-handed.

In her sadness and desolation, Naomi had forgotten that with God, our lives are not over until we see him face-to-face. Even when it seemed to Naomi that there was no hope left, God was still in control. Ruth was about to "accidentally" bump into a man who was a relative of her father-in-law, and that meeting would change human history.

The story of the romance between Ruth and Boaz is a fascinating one. Boaz was much older than Ruth, and he was a wealthy landowner. I know from watching my mother as she tried to make one dollar (or British pound!) do the work of five that it is very hard to raise children as a widow. In the days of Ruth and Naomi, it was desperate. They had no one to care for them. There was no government assistance or welfare plan, but they did have a loving Father watching over them.

As a distant relative, Boaz was not obliged to take care of Naomi or Ruth. He noticed Ruth one day gleaning in his fields. This was a practice allowed to the poor—they could come behind the workers and pick up what had been dropped. Even though it was a recognized practice, Ruth requested permission before she began. When Boaz asked about her, his foreman told him that she was humble, kind, and a hard worker.

God touched Boaz's heart, and he told Ruth not to work in any other field but to work beside his servant girls where she would be safe. He had heard that she had left her own people and pledged her life to Naomi and to the God of Israel, and he blessed her. "May the LORD reward you for all you have done. May your wages be paid in full by the LORD, the God of Israel, under whose wings you have come for shelter" (Ruth 2:12).

In time, Boaz asked Ruth to be his wife. If you have never read the book of Ruth, I highly recommend it to you. It is a story of loss of hope and of redemption. It is a story that points to the birth of Christ.

Soon Ruth gave birth to a little boy named Obed. As Naomi bounced this grandson on her lap, she had no idea that he would grow up and become the father of Jesse, whose son would be King David! These two formerly brokenhearted women are two of only four women (apart from Mary) mentioned in the genealogy of Christ in Matthew 1.

You and I are daughters of the King of kings. We have an enemy who will stop at nothing to destroy all that God loves. It's time we look at our ruby slippers and remember who we really are!

As you look at your life today, you might not feel much like a princess. Perhaps part of that is the image you have of a princess. I am not talking about being a fairy-tale, puffy-dressed diva—far from it! I am talking about what is real, eternally real. You and I are daughters of the King of kings. We have an enemy who will stop at nothing to destroy all that God loves. It's time we look at our ruby slippers and remember who we really are!

9

Cowardly No More!

FREE TO BE GOD'S WARRIOR

"I can still make her my slave, for she does not know how to use her power."
—THE WICKED WITCH OF THE WEST, *THE WONDERFUL WIZARD OF OZ*

*Finally, be strong in the Lord and in his great power. Put on the full
armor of God so that you can fight against the devil's evil tricks. Our
fight is not against people on earth but against the rulers and authorities
and the powers of this world's darkness, against the spiritual powers of
evil in the heavenly world. That is why you need to put on God's full
armor. Then on the day of evil you will be able to stand strong. And
when you have finished the whole fight, you will still be standing.*
—EPHESIANS 6:10–13

Each year, there are two events on my calendar that I dread.
The first is Black Tuesday. Christian and I named it that after one
particularly bad year. We know that it's going to happen each
autumn, so we try to prepare—but how does one prepare for such
a day? I try to get more sleep than usual the week before. I try to eat
well and memorize a psalm, but nothing really takes the edge off.
Black Tuesday is the day that we take our family Christmas photo.

Normal families just send a card or a cute snapshot of their kids that was taken on summer vacation, but not us. Barry wants a professional photo of us all in black turtlenecks or white shirts, yet we all have to look appropriately festive. This is not easy.

If there has ever been a moment in my life when I have wondered if miracles still happen, all doubt was sent packing in the spring of 2005. During our hunting trip in the Texas hills, a friend shot a casual photo of the three of us and Belle sitting on a porch swing. Barry looked at it and commented, "That would make a nice Christmas photo." I heard it with my very own ears, and I had witnesses. Christian wept, I believe that I heard the angels sing, and I doubled my tithe for the next six months!

The other black day is Book Titling Day.

WARRIOR PRINCESS

I wanted to call this book *Warrior Princess*. In my mind's eye I saw a young girl in a long white robe, kneeling at an altar. The figure above her (representing the King) had placed a sword on her shoulder, commissioning her for her role as a warrior princess. Barry wasn't convinced.

"Who is the book for?" he asked.

"It's for women," I responded.

"Young women?" he continued.

"No, of course not; it's for all women. Women of all ages, sizes, and shapes, who love God and want to know that their lives make a difference, that they matter," I said with conviction.

"Do you think a busy single mom or a retired schoolteacher is going to be drawn to that image and understand your heart?" he asked.

Exasperated, I replied, "I'm going out for ice cream!"

It soon became clear to me that Barry had a point. But the heart of the title has never left me, so here goes!

When you think of a princess, what image comes to mind? You might think of Princess Diana and the beauty and humanity she brought to the British royal family. She had such a way of being able to put people at ease, whether it was a child or a patient dying with AIDS. Her accessibility and warmth were initially a shock to the British public.

When I was in my early twenties, I hosted a live music show on the British Broadcasting Network. It was decided one year that we would do a command performance at the Royal Albert Hall in London with Princess Anne as our guest. The evening would benefit her favorite charity, Save the Children. As the host of the show, I met with officials from Buckingham Palace to be taught the appropriate etiquette for meeting a princess. I was told that the first time she addressed me I should call her "Your Royal Highness" and after that, "ma'am."

I practiced curtsying and looking respectful, and I rehearsed her titles over and over. The evening went well, and afterward we all lined up backstage to meet the princess. As she got closer to me, my mind went blank. I couldn't even remember my own name. I thought, *Do I call her "Your Majesty"? No, I think that's the queen.*

Finally, there she was right in front of me. Her palace escort introduced me to her, and I said, "Your Roy— . . . your Maj— . . . oh dear. Hello!" I thought they were going to chop my head off!!

Princess Anne was very sweet. She smiled at me and replied, "Hello to you too!"

Perhaps when you think of a princess, you think of the ones you met as a child through the pages of storybooks or Disney movies. Or Grace Kelly, who went from movie star to royalty when she married Prince Rainier of Monaco and became Princess Grace.

The truth is that until we see Jesus face-to-face, we are at war.

Those images are all part of our popular culture, but they have nothing to do with what it means to be God's princess. Our Father is the King of all kings, and we are his princesses. Not only that, but his kingdom is at war, and we as his daughters have roles to play. The truth is that until we see Jesus face-to-face, we are at war. It's hard to absorb that as we struggle with groceries and car-pool lines, but it is the truth. We are not living in a time of peace, even though we are in relationship with the Prince of Peace.

THE DAY THAT CHANGED AMERICA

Much attention has always been given to wars being waged around the world. But on the dreadful day of September 11, 2001, everything changed. It suddenly became shockingly real to Americans that our enemies could walk right up to our front door and enter uninvited. As long as the terrorists were "out there," they didn't seem so real; but as we watched them change the landscape of our nation, they changed the landscape of our hearts.

I have no desire to minimize the danger of the times we live in, but I do want to remind us of something that is easy to forget. Our human enemies have one life to live, and then it is over. They can plot and plan to terrorize the world, but God is still in ultimate control over how much evil he will allow to be poured out on us.

There is, however, a far greater enemy than those featured on the nightly news. God has warned us about this enemy, yet most of the time, we think of him as "out there." But the reality is that Satan is always nearby. As the apostle Peter warns us, "Control yourselves and be careful! The devil, your enemy, goes around like a roaring lion looking for someone to eat. Refuse to give in to him, by standing strong in your faith" (1 Peter 5:8–9).

You might wonder what this passage about spiritual warfare has to say to us on the subject of God's dream for our lives. I would love to answer that.

God Speaks

I believe that God is the author of every good thing on this earth. I see him as I look at Rembrandt's paintings or read the works of Dostoyevsky. I see his hand in a painting that my son gives me or in the dry humor of Charles Schultz's comic strip *Charlie Brown and Friends*. If we have ears to hear and eyes to see, God shows up everywhere. As you know by now, I see his hand and heart in children's literature, especially *The Wonderful Wizard of Oz*.

When the Wicked Witch of the West looked down at Dorothy's feet and saw that she was wearing the ruby slippers, she began to tremble with fear. She considered running away from Dorothy until one thing became clear to her: Dorothy had no idea how much power she had. The Witch realized that as long as Dorothy was unaware of her own power, she would not contest the Witch's commands.

> *The Witch realized that as long as Dorothy was unaware of her own power, she would not contest the Witch's commands.*

I think that is a fabulous analogy of a deep spiritual truth. We have an enemy who wants to crush our God-given dreams. He knows that because of the finished work of Christ on the cross, he is powerless against us. But he has one thing on his side: we don't know who we are. We have forgotten that because of Jesus and the life blood he poured out on our behalf, we are covered.

Marked with a Kiss

Before Dorothy embarks on her journey down the yellow brick road, the kind Witch of the North kisses her on her forehead. Her touch leaves a round, shimmering mark behind. Dorothy can't see it, but the Wicked Witch of the West can. Although the Witch threatened to beat her, she was actually afraid to lay a hand on the girl.

Does that remind you of another story?

Cowardly No More!

THE ANGEL OF DEATH

We read in the book of Exodus that when Moses was eighty years old, God told him to return to Egypt—it was time to set his people free. Pharaoh refused to listen, and so began a series of ten terrible plagues inflicted on the land and people of Egypt. Terrible as they were, none compared to the final assault.

The last plague struck the firstborn male of every animal and every family. From the firstborn son of Pharaoh to the firstborn son of the slave girl working in the fields, every family would be visited by the angel of death at midnight. No one was exempt.

God instructed Moses to tell each Israelite family to take a one-year-old, flawless lamb and slaughter it. The blood of the lamb should be painted on the top and sides of the doorframes of their homes. They were to eat the lamb with their walking shoes on because, come morning, it would be time to leave. When God spills blood, things change. The people were moving out of bondage into freedom. It was time for the children of Israel to dream again.

When you have come into relationship with God through Christ, you are marked with the blood of Christ for life.

The angel of death passed over every home and field in Egypt that dreadful night, and where there was the mark of lamb's blood, he passed over. I cannot imagine the wails that pierced the air as thousands of families faced the loss of their firstborn. Many dreams died that night.

The spotless lambs whose blood covered the children of God

were a picture of Christ, the spotless Lamb of God, whose blood would be spilled to cover us. When you have come into relationship with God through Christ, you are marked with the blood of Christ for life. God knows it, the angels see it, and the devil fears it—but sometimes we forget.

When We Substitute Doing for Dreaming

Unless we grasp that as God's daughters we can experience the amazing dream he has for our lives, we will have missed the true call of God. Let me suggest a few reasons we use to convince ourselves that we cannot stand with our heads held high, wielding the sword of the Spirit:

I'm not good enough.
I've made too many mistakes.
When I get my life in order, then I'll be worthy.
I'm not strong.
I'm afraid.
It's too late.

When the angel of death passed over homes marked with the blood of the lamb, he did not once ask who was in the home or how well they had behaved that day. He didn't ask if they had kept every vow that they had made to God. He didn't ask if they were fearless and full of faith. All of that was irrelevant. All he needed to see was the blood of the lamb.

How much time have you wasted wondering if you are good enough to dream big for God?

How much time and joy have you lost because you allowed the enemy to convince you that you are weak and vulnerable?

> *How much time have you wasted wondering if you are good enough to dream big for God?*

You are a daughter of the King of kings, a warrior princess covered in the righteousness of Christ, and hell trembles when even one of us gets it.

A WARRIOR PRINCESS NAMED DEBBIE

From 1987 through 1992, I was cohost of *The 700 Club with Pat Robertson*. During my tenure there, I met a young woman who forever changed how I dream and how I fight as God's warrior princess.

I picked up the first letter in my pile of correspondence that day and got no further. I was arrested by the brutal honesty of this young fighter. Her name was Debbie, and she said that she watched our show two or three times a day. Sometimes it helped her, and sometimes she wanted to take off her shoe and throw it through the television screen.

My first thought was, *Why would anyone watch the same show two or three times a day?* Her letter went on to explain that she had been diagnosed with multiple sclerosis and had cancer in her bones. Her question was a simple one: "Why do you only show the stories of people who have been healed? Why don't you air pieces about those who have not been healed yet still love God?"

I was riveted by her questions and wanted to know more, so I called the number she had included in her note. We talked for two hours that first day and went on to become close friends until her death. Debbie changed my life. She taught me that some of God's most noble warriors are fragile. They barely make a footprint in the snow, but every step they take is a huge victory.

Some of God's most noble warriors are fragile. They barely make a footprint in the snow, but every step they take is a huge victory.

Debbie knew that she was dying. She knew that God could heal her, but it didn't seem that was his plan. Debbie never stopped dreaming. What was clear to her was that although some of her dreams might not be fulfilled until heaven, it made them no less worthy of dreaming right now.

I saw through Debbie's pain and joy that many of us have traded God's dream for our lives for fantasizing. In a subtle twist of truth, we can easily fall prey to the false assumption that ease of circumstances is an indication of the pleasure of God. If that were true, then Debbie was lost—but she was far from lost. She was found as few know they are found. She dared to dream the biggest dream of all. She dreamed that no matter how things seem to be, no matter how many petty victories our enemy appears to win, God's warrior princesses are victorious because their Prince holds the keys of death and hell.

There were many moments before her death when it seemed as

if Debbie was about to succumb to the brutalities of her illness. She would be rushed to the hospital, fighting for breath and in extreme pain. After each physical battering, I would ask her, "Where was God during the most extreme moments?" Her answer was always the same: "Right there. He was right there holding me so close, it was as if I heard him breathe for me."

Through Debbie's life and death, I came to a place of personal conviction that to be able to experience God's dream for our lives, we have to trust God and not let fear rule the day. Fear will have its moments, but it will not have its way.

Fear will have its moments, but it will not have its way.

Debbie was one of God's daughters, a princess. I count it one of the great privileges of my life that I was able for even a brief time to walk side-by-side with this noble warrior princess.

That takes us to the edge of this next part. Dorothy and her traveling companions were well on their way to the Emerald City. What they did not know was how the journey would change them and their dreams.

PART TWO

Inside the Emerald City

HOW OUR DREAMS CHANGE

10

Why Would You Want to Go Back?

CHANGED AS WE ARE MADE WHOLE

"Why would you wish to see Oz?" he asked.
"I want him to send me back to Kansas . . ." Dorothy answered.
—THE WONDERFUL WIZARD OF OZ

Don't become so well-adjusted to your culture that you fit into
it without even thinking. Instead, fix your attention on God.
You'll be changed from the inside out . . . Unlike the culture around you,
always dragging you down to its level of immaturity, God brings
the best out of you, develops well-formed maturity in you.
—ROMANS 12:2 MSG

Their names are Trinny and Susannah, and they can bring the strongest woman to tears. Their show is *What Not to Wear*, and it airs on BBC America. The first time I watched this television show, I cringed as an unsuspecting British woman put her life under the microscope of these self-appointed fashion gurus.

On this show, husbands or children nominate their wives or

moms as candidates for a complete makeover. They have to convince the producers of the show that the woman they are recom-
mending has all the fashion sense of a drunken hippopotamus.

If the producers consider the nominee a likely contender, they
stalk her with a hidden camera, capturing shots of her in her most
unflattering moments. Then Trinny and Susannah show up at the
candidate's home or workplace with a camera crew and announce
to this sacrificial lamb that she has been chosen to have her life
revamped.

Some of the women are excited, but those with more sense are
terrified. If they accept the offer, then the fun begins. First off, they
have the joy of watching the tape that was filmed in secret. It is usually awful! The show's producers show no mercy, and every bad
angle possible is presented full-screen for the whole world to see.

If the woman in question has a larger "sit-upon" than might be
desired, then that is what they show. If her skirt is too tight or her
bra is the wrong size, the camera zooms in with Machiavellian
delight. It is humiliating!

Then Trinny and Susannah go through the woman's wardrobe
and throw most of her clothes away. Having told her everything
she is doing is wrong, they then give the woman the equivalent of
about eight thousand dollars and release her to stores, with the
cameras in tow. It is agony to watch. The woman usually staggers
from store to store with a dazed expression as if she has just been
released from the hospital after a full-frontal lobotomy.

"If the show is so terrible, then why do you watch?" you
might ask.

Well, it's like a traffic accident: you don't want to look, but you
can't help yourself. Also, having watched the first few moments of

an episode, I feel compelled to stay with it and hope for a happy ending. After all, I have watched this woman's public mortification, so I feel compelled to be there at the end to cheer her rebirth. Sometimes I get so involved that I find myself talking to the television.

"No! Don't choose that—they said not to wear pink."

"Oh good grief, they will be furious with you if you buy flat shoes."

"Look out—they're coming. Pick up something yellow quick!"

What's interesting is that behind the rhetoric, Trinny and Susannah actually have very tender hearts. Underneath their brutal honesty, they appear to have a genuine desire to help women who have given up on themselves. One show in particular touched me deeply.

A New Beginning

The show held open auditions for any woman who felt that she needed some help to get back into life. They were asked to come in either their best outfit for a date if they were single or their most professional look for a job interview if they were considering reentering the workforce.

It was fascinating to see what the various women chose to wear. One woman came in a dress that looked to be at least three sizes too small, two feet too short, and forty years too late.

They lined up the final eight women and then narrowed their selection to two. I was surprised and delighted by their choice. Instead of choosing the more flamboyant and outrageous ones who might have made for an entertaining show, they chose the two quietest ones.

One lady was obviously brokenhearted that her husband had left her, and she hadn't bought anything new for herself in years. The other lady was from Scotland. She was quiet and conservative. She looked at Trinny and Susannah as if they were exotic birds that no self-respecting sparrow would be seen with.

As is the show's typical procedure, the fashion gurus went through the Scottish lady's wardrobe and tossed 90 percent of it to one side for Goodwill. She was horrified and kept rescuing items from the rapidly growing pile. She was obviously very distressed by the whole process, and I found myself wondering why she had applied to go on the show at all.

Finally, it was time for her to go shopping for a new wardrobe. She picked up a few things and headed for a changing room. I don't know how long it was in real time, since the show is taped, but it became clear to the watching audience that she wasn't coming out. One of the girls went in to see what was wrong, and the cameraperson followed.

She was facing a full-length mirror, tears streaming down her face. When she was able to talk, she said that she had no idea who she was anymore. Her despair was clear: how can you choose new clothes when you have no self to put them on?

I watched with tears rolling down my face too. I felt such empathy for this woman. It would be ridiculous to tell her to dream big; she had forgotten how to dream at all. Whatever dream she'd once had for her life was no longer intact. For whatever reason, life had told her in no uncertain terms that she was fooling herself to think her dreams could ever come true.

Why Would You Want to Go Back?

CHILDLIKE DREAMS

When I was a teenager, I wanted so badly to be tall. As I looked at my family tree, which with all respect is more of a bush than a tree, it wasn't looking good. So I made a deal with God. I told him that if I woke up the next morning and was four inches taller, then in return I would be a missionary to China. God obviously decided that China had enough problems and left me where I was.

Have you ever been there?

When you look back at your childhood, what did you dream for yourself?

If your dreams changed, when—and why—did they change?

Did you exchange them for better dreams? Or did you just stop dreaming?

> *When you look back at your childhood, what did you dream for yourself?*

IF ONLY . . .

Dorothy dreamed of a world where there would be no more sorrow or disappointment: "Where troubles melt like lemon drops away above the chimney tops, that's where you'll find me."[1] When she landed in Oz, however, it became clear that far from melting like lemon drops, her troubles were piling up like unpaid bills. Dreams can be disappointing.

Childhood dreams are often the stuff of fairy tales and revolve around a place or a person or a look:

If she would be my best friend, then I would be happy.
If I were taller, then I would be happy.
If I were prettier, then I would have more friends.
If he were my daddy, then my life would be wonderful.

Just like the wonderfully naïve Glinda in the musical *Wicked*, as children we often believe that being popular is what we really want. If you dig a little deeper, though, what lies behind that belief? Popularity in itself can't be the draw; it has to be more than that. My guess is that it is what we believe popularity says about someone:

If you are popular, you are loved.
If you are popular, you are worth loving.
If you are popular, you will never be alone.

A Dream Lost

The camera pulled away and gave our Scottish friend a few moments to gather herself. As the show went to commercial break, I thought about the vast number of women I have met over the last few years who could have been the one standing in front of the full-length mirror—women who have lost their way or been abandoned on their path. Before we move on to a new dream and a new life, it is wise to deal with the disappointment of the old.

Perhaps when your dreams have died, you need a change of view.

Why Would You Want to Go Back?

If a woman has built all her dreams around being someone's wife and suddenly finds herself divorced, what does that do to her dreams?

If a woman has lived to be a mother and discovers that she can't have children, where does she go from that cliff's edge?

Perhaps when your dreams have died, you need a change of view.

It Depends on Where You Are Standing

When I lived in London, I decided to take a trip to Land's End. The scenery is spectacular with magnificent cliffs overlooking the Atlantic Ocean. It's quite breathtaking. You need a good head for heights to be able to go anywhere near the edge of these fabled cliffs.

As I stood there that day, looking out across the ocean to the French coast, I had a little epiphany. I discovered that my position altered my perspective significantly. If I stood with my back to England, looking down over the jagged edges to the water below, I had come to the end. There was nowhere else to go. But if I turned around and had my back to the ocean, I looked out across the lush fields of Cornwall and had the whole country in front of me. I was just beginning, and I could go almost anywhere.

I think it is the same with our dreams. When a dream dies, we can fix our gaze solely on what lies behind in the dust or, with God's help, we can turn around and dream a new dream.

I believe that dreams should be honored even if they were foolish or unfulfilled. When I look back at some of the things I dreamed for as a child, it is easy to ridicule or dismiss them. I think we do too much of that as women. We are so critical of ourselves. My prayer for you today at this place in your journey is for a fresh experience of the grace of God. You would not be the woman you are today, with all that is beautiful and kind and strong in you, if you had not come along the very path that you did.

Broken dreams should be given time to be mourned. We live in such a fast-paced culture that we often don't give our hearts time to catch up with our bodies. I wonder how many sicknesses are actually our bodies telling us that we are not doing well. When we take time to mourn what has come to an end, then we are ready for God to meet us with the next step in our journey.

TURN AROUND, HAGAR

In the book of Genesis, we are not told how Hagar came into Abraham and Sarah's household. It is clear that she was an Egyptian slave, but whether she was sold by poverty-stricken parents or captured during a raid on Egypt and sold by traders is not clear. She was, however, Sarah's slave; she was not a concubine. Sarah had become desperate that she was not able to conceive a child. God had promised them children, but the clock was ticking on. At this point in the story, Sarah was seventy-five years old, and Abraham was eighty-five. So she told her husband that he should sleep with Hagar, and through this surrogacy Sarah would become a mother, which was an accepted practice.

What we *don't* read about in Scripture is what must have been going on behind the scenes.

In any marriage where the couple is unable to conceive, the

inevitable question is, whose problem is it? When Sarah gave her servant to Abraham, Hagar became pregnant immediately. Part of Sarah must have been thrilled, but it was clear now to everyone in the household that the problem was Sarah's. That had to be a bitter pill to swallow. What made it much worse was that Hagar's attitude toward Sarah became demeaning and derisive. We read that Hagar began to despise her mistress.

Sarah was stuck. This was her idea, after all, yet it had turned into a nightmare. When she complained to Abraham, he reminded her that Hagar was her maid and that she should handle this herself.

Sarah's way of handling the situation was to make life miserable for Hagar. It must have been pretty bad for Hagar, because she ran away. That would have been the last choice of a poor, pregnant slave. From the road she took, she may have been trying to get back to Egypt, but this would have been an impossible journey for a pregnant woman to take by herself.

The next thing we read about her is that she is resting by a stream in the middle of the wilderness. Hagar is in a terrible place. She is carrying a child, but she has no place to go, and her future looks bleak. She must have thought that she and her unborn child would die in the wilderness. But then God stepped in!

Genesis 16:7 says that while Hagar was resting by the stream, she was approached by "the Angel of the LORD" (NKJV). Many scholars believe that it was God himself who appeared to Hagar. This is certainly a very intimate term describing God's personal interaction with a human being. It is the first time in Scripture that this phrase is used. Later, when God calls on Abraham as he is about to bury a dagger in Isaac's heart, he appears as the angel of the Lord (Genesis 22:11). When God speaks to Moses through the burning bush, he appears as the angel of the Lord (Exodus 3:2). But I think it very touching that this term is used first not only to a woman but to a runaway pregnant slave.

The angel's message to Hagar was a mixed blessing. He promised life, but he also promised strife. He told her that her son "shall be a wild man; his hand shall be against every man, and every man's hand against him" (Genesis 16:12 NKJV).

Almost every morning when I read the paper or listen to the news, I see the legacy of Ishmael (Hagar's son) and Isaac (Sarah's son), both of whom received promises from God. Through Isaac, we have the Jewish people who inhabit Israel. Through Ishmael, we have the Arab people who populate most of the Middle East today.

I believe 100 percent in the sovereignty of God, that nothing happens that has not first passed through his merciful hands. However, I do find myself wondering how human history would have been different if Sarah had waited on the dream God had for her life instead of coming up with a plan of her own.

> When we have come to the end of ourselves, God is waiting to give us a new dream.

The angel of the Lord told Hagar to turn around and go back to her mistress and submit to her. God promised her that he would multiply her descendants. We read that Hagar clung onto that promise. She called God *El Roi*, which means "The God who sees" (v. 13). Hagar returned to Sarah and gave birth to Ishmael.

What is clear to me from Hagar's story is that God is always watching over us. When we have come to the end of ourselves, God is waiting to give us a new dream.

TRANSFORMED

I switched my attention back to the television screen for the big reveal. Trinny and Susannah were excited to show off what they had done with my Scottish friend. It was quite a transformation. Her hair was cut and dyed a new shade of chestnut brown. She was in a beautifully tailored suit. She looked quite lovely.

As I recall, she was radiant and clearly shocked that she had that beauty in her all along. It was just waiting to be recognized.

As I cheered for this beautiful woman, I said a prayer for her—a prayer that I say for you today too: "Father God, I thank you for this woman. I thank you for her courage and honesty, for her tears and for her smile. I pray today that she will know you, the One who created her and who has always loved her. I ask that she will see herself as you see her, beautiful always. May she feel your smile today. Amen."

11

A Very Bad Wizard

CHANGED BY DISAPPOINTMENT

"I think you are a very bad man," said Dorothy.
"Oh no, my dear; I'm really a very good man; but I'm a very bad wizard."
—The Wonderful Wizard of Oz

Create in me a pure heart, God, and make my spirit right again. Do not send
me away from you or take your Holy Spirit away from me. Give me back the
joy of your salvation. Keep me strong by giving me a willing spirit.
—Psalm 51:10–12

Their moment had finally come. Dorothy, Toto, the Scarecrow, the Tin Woodsman, and the Cowardly Lion were ushered once more into the presence of the great Oz.

Their first encounter with the great wizard had been decidedly disappointing. Instead of granting their requests, he had asked them to do something for him. He asked them to kill the Wicked Witch of the West and bring her broomstick back as proof of her demise. This seemed an impossible task. Not only impossible but very distasteful.

Dorothy said that she had no desire to kill anyone—not even to

So far they had learned one very important thing: they did better when they were together than each one alone.

get home. The Cowardly Lion explained that he certainly couldn't do it; the very thought was terrifying. The Scarecrow thought he might be willing to do it but was too much of a fool to get it right. The Tin Woodsman pointed out that he didn't have the heart for it!

It was clear, though, that if their dreams were to come true, the four friends would have to try. So far they had learned one very important thing: they did better when they were together than each one alone. So they set off.

UNDER HER SPELL

The Wicked Witch of the West was an unusual creature to behold. Not only was she a fairly arresting shade of green, but she had only one eye. That eye, however, was as powerful as a telescope. As soon as she saw the travelers approach her kingdom, she sent her troop of winged monkeys out to stop them. Her directions were to kill them all except for the lion. She intended to harness him and use him as a horse.

When the monkeys encountered Dorothy, they knew that they could not kill her. They said, "She is protected by the Power of Good, and that is greater than the Power of Evil."[1]

They attacked the Scarecrow and the Tin Woodsman and left them for dead. Then they carried Dorothy and the Cowardly Lion back to the Witch. The witch was shocked when she saw the mark on Dorothy's forehead, and when she saw the ruby slippers on Dorothy's feet, she became furious. She wanted them more than anything, because she understood their power. As we saw in a previous chapter, the Wicked Witch knew that she could not actually harm Dorothy, even though she threatened her constantly.

The Wicked Witch was cruel to the Cowardly Lion and had him tied up outside with no food. At night when the Wicked Witch was asleep, Dorothy would slip out and take food to her friend. After he had eaten, she would lay her head down on his mane to comfort him, as all good friends would do.

Friends Are Friends Forever

I stopped reading at that point in the story; I didn't want to rush past it. In that moment, as I imagined Dorothy bringing food to her friend and lying down beside him, I felt a deep longing.

I think so many of us are lonely for that kind of vulnerable companionship when life is not working. It is much easier for us as women, Christians in particular, to rally around one another when life is good. But when our prayers don't seem to be answered and God appears silent, we pull away. We don't know what to say.

We are sometimes afraid to say what we really feel because we fear it will be misunderstood and seen as a lack of faith. But Dorothy and the

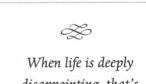

When life is deeply disappointing, that's when we need each other more than ever.

Cowardly Lion had learned that when life is deeply disappointing, that's when we need each other more than ever.

ALONE AGAIN, NATURALLY

In my book *I'm Not Wonder Woman, but God Made Me Wonderful,* I share a story about my friendship with Marilyn Meberg.[2] Marilyn is one of the core members of the Women of Faith speaking team. The moment I met her, I knew that we would be friends. She has a zany sense of humor and a very tender heart. I didn't know it then, but God had ordained our friendship to teach me one of the greatest lessons in life. One of the gifts of relationship is that it shows us where we are strong and where we are weak.

In the early spring of 2002, Marilyn and I were asked to fly to Las Vegas to promote an upcoming conference. We had interviews in the morning and a meeting that night at a local church, but the afternoon was free. I told Marilyn that I might take a look at the shops, and she said that sounded fun.

When we got back to our hotel after the interviews, instead of asking her if she wanted to come with me, I headed off by myself. Part of that was that I tend to be a loner. But part of it was that I didn't want to ask her to come in case that would make her feel obliged to join me. After all, she might not want to spend her free time with me.

I have carried a strong cord of rejection from my childhood that tends to vote others off the island before they ask me to leave. It was only later that Marilyn told me that the experience had hurt her. After I asked her to forgive me, I said to her, "Marilyn, I don't know how to be a good friend, but I want to be. Will you help me?"

In facing that disappointing truth about myself, I was able to allow someone into a very vulnerable, shame-filled place. It was a life-changing moment for me. In the months and years that have followed, Marilyn and I have become very close and have enjoyed a depth of friendship that I had not experienced before. We give each other permission to bring all that we are to the table. We share our joys and our disappointments; we laugh and cry and celebrate together the gift of friendship.

A Twist in the Road

As I put my Oz book aside for a moment, I not only remembered the longing I once felt for close companionship, but I also felt deep gratitude for the way God is answering that longing. A recent crisis showed me how faithful God is to help us when we admit that we need help.

For years, Marilyn has suffered with on and off severe back pain and numbness in her right leg. In February 2006, instead of dissipating, it became more severe. She consulted a neurosurgeon who told her that she needed surgery immediately.

Within two days, she was in the hospital. Luci Swindoll, Mary Graham, Ney Bailey, Pat Wenger, and I sat in the family waiting room. In this room was a computer screen displaying the names of each patient undergoing surgery that morning. Beside each name, symbols appeared indicating what was happening. When the surgeon made his first cut, a little scalpel appeared. It was a scary moment as we sat together and prayed for our dear friend.

Just before noon, the surgeon appeared and told us that the surgery had gone well. He said that Marilyn had woken up with a silly grin on her face. (I didn't have the heart to tell him that she always had a silly grin on her face!)

During her presurgery visits, the doctor told Marilyn that when she came out of the anesthetic she should be pain free. But he discovered that the herniated disc had been pressing on the nerve for so long that it would probably take some time for it to recover. He told us that we could go to Marilyn's room and wait for her.

A young nurse popped her head round the door and seemed surprised to see all five of us in the room. "It really should just be family in here!" she said.

"We are family!" we replied in unison.

Then another, more officious nurse looked in and said sternly, "Only two in a room! We can only have two in a room!"

We just looked at her as if we didn't speak English.

It was so good to see Marilyn when they wheeled her in. She looked good and pain free. The doctor had said that at three o'clock she should try to walk. He wanted her to be able to walk up and down the corridor before he released her to go home.

At three o'clock, Marilyn swung her feet over to the side of the bed and very carefully stood up. I will never forget the look on Marilyn's face when her legs took the weight of her body. The pain was so intense she cried out loud and almost crumbled. For two hours she tried to walk, but the pain was excruciating.

"This is worse than before," she moaned as she lay back down on her side. We all wept. There was silence in the room. It was one of those moments in life when there is nothing to say. I went over to Marilyn and put my arms around her and held her. All I could say was, "I am so sorry. I am so sorry."

I am happy to report that the nerve has recovered, and the pain is now gone. In the days following the surgery, we took turns bringing meals and staying with Marilyn so that she wouldn't be alone. We would often talk through the events of that day and how hard it was to face the bitter disappointment of a dream dashed and the potential of a situation that was worse than before. Marilyn told me one of the things that helped her most was when I held her. She said, "You didn't pretend that everything was all right; you just said that you were so sorry."

I tell that story not to indicate that I should be your visitor of choice at your next crisis but to show how good God is in helping us change in places where we are stuck. The old Sheila would have wanted to hold Marilyn but decided to stand back in case it was the wrong thing to do. What I understand now is that in the face of life's many disappointments, there is no "right" thing to do. We give what we have, and that is ourselves. It is the gift of our presence.

What's the Point of Disappointment?

Disappointment can either alienate us from one another or bring us together. Admitting that life does not always work out the way we'd hoped or prayed for does not diminish the reality of God's abilities or his love, but it does provide an opportunity for us to express that love to one another. Sometimes we need to remind ourselves that we are not called to be God's PR agents but to be his heart.

I wonder if one of the uses of disappointment is to redirect our hearts and minds. What if what we are really longing for is home, when God will finally make everything all right? Maybe our real disappointment lies not in the specific incident (or lack of it) but rather in the stinging recognition that all is not well. We all put different words to this song of longing in our souls, but the melody seems to be universal. As my dear friend Luci Swindoll says, "Nothing works!"

We are not called to be God's PR agents but to be his heart.

One of the realities of life is that even when we do get what we want, that in itself can be disappointing because it's not as perfect as we thought it would be. One of my favorite Woody Allen quotes is, "It's not the despair that gets you; it's the hope." I understand that. We have self-preservation built into our souls, and when it's clear that something is going badly, we pull up our bootstraps and prepare for the storm ahead. We think, *I can do this.*

What takes us by surprise is when we believe something will really work this time. We invest ourselves body and soul. When the rug is all of a sudden pulled out from underneath us like a tablecloth trick, it's very difficult to recover. Part of our upset is that it didn't work, and part of it is anger at ourselves for being foolish enough to believe it would.

The Bible has a lot to say about hope. Proverbs 13:12 tells us, "Hope deferred makes the heart sick, but when the desire comes, it is a tree of life" (NKJV). And the apostle Paul wrote to the church in Rome, "We also have joy with our troubles, because we know that these troubles produce patience. And patience produces character, and character produces hope. And this hope will never disappoint us, because God has poured out his love to fill our hearts" (Romans 5:3–5).

There seems to be a huge gap between the realities expressed in Proverbs 13 and the encouragement to hope that Paul presents to the church in Rome. We read that hope deferred makes the heart sick, but when the desire comes it is a tree of life to us. But what if the fulfillment of the desire never comes? What if the door is permanently closed on this side of seeing God face-to-face?

I think of one of my dearest friends who longed to be a mother. For years she and her husband tried to conceive, only to discover that she had gone into early menopause. Accepting this they then tried to adopt, only to be told they were now too old to adopt. The door that slammed in her face seems final and cruel.

Deep disappointment, as opposed to inconvenience, always seems to fall into the area of relationships—whether it's with ourselves, with others, or even with God.

GIVING UP THE RED CAPE

During the process of writing *I'm Not Wonder Woman, but God Made Me Wonderful*, I realized how reluctant I had been to give up the cape and boots of a superhero. I wanted to be Wonder Woman, never needing help or rescue. I felt that gave me value in God's eyes and worth to others. It also protected me.

When I met Barry, he began to scale the wall that I had built around my heart. Then with God's help I began to take it down, brick by brick. As God's light has begun to flood in, I am seeing things that I have never seen before.

While I was growing up, if you had asked me what my greatest sin was, I would have told you that it was pride. I was proud of myself and thought that God should be proud of me too. After all, I tried so hard to get it all right. I stayed away from all of the "big" sins. It was in the psychiatric hospital that I finally began to realize that I have nothing to bring to the table apart from my relationship with Jesus Christ.

We come poor and naked, and in Christ we are made rich and are clothed in his righteousness.

What I didn't realize at the time was that although I rejected my foolish pride, I had exchanged it for something equally self-serving. Instead of accepting God's grace and forgiveness for thinking I was the perfect Christian, I began to beat myself up for being so presumptuous as to think that I could earn God's love.

Pride is insidious and can easily change disguises to resemble humility. But it is always about us. We are either too good or too bad. It is so hard to embrace the fact that regardless of our efforts, we are simply disappointing. We'll never get it right on our own steam. That's why grace is so hard for many of us to accept: it says that we have absolutely nothing to offer. We come poor and naked, and in Christ we are made rich and are clothed in his righteousness.

At long last, I am beginning to live in that grace. So I have stopped beating up this little girl who grew up Sheila Davina

Walsh. Underneath the red cape and the superhero stunts for God was just a child who wanted God to love her like a daddy would love his little girl. That's okay, because he does.

LOOK, DAD!

I see Christian do it with his dad, and I love it. During the writing of this manuscript, Christian learned to ride a bike. Although he is almost ten years old, he had spent more time on a skateboard than a bike, so his old bike still had training wheels on it. It didn't bother him at all until he spent the night with one of his best friends from school and suddenly became aware that he couldn't do something that his friend could. The following day he said to me, "Mom, can I get a new bike?" I looked at his bike to see if we could just remove the training wheels, but it was far too small.

There is a fabulous bike store just a few blocks away from where we live, so Christian and I went there the next day after school. They had bikes in every color imaginable. He sat on several to see how they would feel and finally settled on one. The sales assistant asked him if he knew how to ride. Christian told him that he didn't, as he was more of a skateboarder.

"Then you will learn in fifteen minutes," the assistant assured him. "It's all about balance. If you can skateboard, you have good balance."

I could have shot him! In fairness, the sales assistant was trying to be encouraging; but I was listening to him through the ears of my perfectionist son, who now believed that if he didn't get it right in less than fifteen minutes he was a failure. We bought a helmet and gloves and drove home.

"Let's go out now, Mom!" he urged. "Then I'll be able to ride when Dad gets home."

We sat down for a moment in the kitchen. I did not want to rain on his parade, but I wanted to make sure his parade lasted for more than two minutes. "Sweet pea, I think that it's possible that you might learn how to ride a bike in fifteen minutes, but it took me a week. So if you don't get it right away, don't be hard on yourself," I said.

"All righty then!" he replied, but in his mind he was already flying like the wind.

Ten minutes later, we were back in the house. "I'll never be able to do this; it's too hard!" he wailed. "I knew that I wouldn't be able to do it!"

Once more we sat together and unpacked a picnic of grace. I'm sure there will be many picnics ahead.

SAVED!

Life on earth is by its very job description disappointing. Adam and Eve were the first human beings to be faced with that reality. To Eve, God said, "I will cause you to have much trouble when you are pregnant, and when you give birth to children, you will have great pain. You will greatly desire your husband, but he will rule over you" (Genesis 3:16).

Adam's legacy was equally bleak. God told him, "I will put a curse on the ground, and you will have to work very hard for your food. In pain you will eat its food all the days of your life. The ground will produce thorns and weeds for you, and you will eat the plants of the field. You will sweat and work hard for your food" (vv. 17–19).

Even at that moment of the greatest disappointment encountered by human beings as they were forced to leave the Garden of Eden, God whispered how he would save us all. To the serpent Satan, he said, "One of her descendants will crush your head, and you will bite his heel" (v. 15).

Jesus Christ, the Son of God, would be born as one of us. He would taste the bitter disappointments of this life and allow the serpent to bite his heel. Even as he lay down, poisoned by the wound, our salvation was underway.

12

The Scarecrow's Gift

CHANGED BY THE LOVE OF GOD

*"Take out my straw and scatter it over the little girl and the dog and
the lion," he said to the Woodsman, "and the bees cannot sting them."*

—THE SCARECROW, *THE WONDERFUL WIZARD OF OZ*

*Surely He has borne our griefs and carried our sorrows; yet we esteemed
Him stricken, smitten by God, and afflicted. But He was wounded for
our transgressions, He was bruised for our iniquities; the chastisement
for our peace was upon Him, and by His stripes we are healed.*

—ISAIAH 53:4–5 NKJV

"Why is it so dark, Mom?" Christian asked as we took our
seats.

"Because it's Good Friday," I answered. "The darkness in the
sanctuary reminds us of how dark it must have been for Jesus on
the night he was betrayed."

"But we won't be able to read the words of the hymns,"
Christian whispered, determined to find a problem.

"I'm sure they'll bring the lights up for that," I assured him.
"Just listen to the music until the service starts."

Instead of our usual full orchestra, there was a string quartet playing quietly on the platform. The strings played the melody to "Beneath the Cross of Jesus," one of my favorite hymns from childhood:

Beneath the cross of Jesus I fain would take my stand,
The shadow of a mighty rock within a weary land;
A home within the wilderness, a rest upon the way,
From the burning of the noontide heat, and the burden
of the day.[1]

As we sat in the quiet darkness, I tried to imagine what it must have been like to wake up on that Thursday morning, the day before Jesus was betrayed.

THURSDAY MORNING

It was an important day in Jerusalem. It was the first day of the Feast of Unleavened Bread, when the Passover lamb is slaughtered. It was a day of remembrance and thanksgiving for all that God had done for his people. Jerusalem was busy, noisy, and crowded. The bleating of the Passover lambs being brought into the city to be slaughtered filled the air. There was much to see and do that day, but the clock was ticking, and everything that had once represented *normal* was about to change forever.

Not one of Jesus's disciples understood that, by nightfall, their lives would be radically altered. To them, it was another Passover, though perhaps a little tenser than usual. Jesus was saying some things that were making their religious leaders furious, but the crowds loved him. They had seen that just a few days ago. The crowd went wild when Jesus rode into Jerusalem on a donkey. It had been quite a day. Even Jesus seemed different.

Last week had been amazing. When some of the leaders told the people to stop shouting, Jesus said that if they did, the very rocks would cry out. It was exciting; things were on the move.

One by one, the twelve disciples woke up on Thursday morning.

PETER

I wonder what went through Peter's mind as he got out of bed. Was his back acting up again? All those years as a fisherman hoisting heavy nets after a good night's catch had surely taken a toll.

He was worried about Jesus because he talked so much these days about dying. He said it had to be, that there was no other way. Peter had pulled him aside one day and said, "God save you from those things, Lord! Those things will never happen to you!" But Jesus had turned on him. He had called Peter "Satan" and told him that he wasn't helping at all. That cut deep. All Peter wanted to do was to be there for Jesus. He believed in him. He knew that he was the one who had been promised. Peter had seen so much recently.

There was that unforgettable moment on the mountain. It was just the four of them: Jesus, Peter, James, and John. Peter saw it with his own eyes: Jesus's face had changed. It shone like the sun. There were others with him, but they were not like anyone Peter had ever encountered before. This was a miracle, a gift from God that Peter got to see with his own eyes. How could he ever tell anyone? No one would believe him, for standing with Jesus—standing there and talking to him—were Moses and Elijah.

Who ever thought a fisherman would see such a sight! Peter wanted to do something, to build something to remember this moment. But Jesus said no. He told them not to tell anyone until everything was over. What did that mean, and how would he know when everything was over?

Things were changing too fast for Peter, who knew what today might hold.

JOHN

Was John, the beloved disciple, sad when he awoke that morning? He had to be, for he was close to Jesus. More than the others, he loved Jesus out of a pure heart. He knew that Jesus's time was ticking down. He could feel it. He could see it in his friend's eyes. When Jesus prayed for them, it was as if he were saying good-bye. What would he do if Jesus were taken from them? What would any of them do? What about Jesus's mother? She loved her son so fiercely.

JUDAS

What was Thursday morning like for Judas? Did he sleep with the money under his mat? How heavy did the bag of silver feel that day? Thirty pieces of silver—the price of a slave. Did he think that the religious leaders should have paid more? Was that all Jesus's life was worth? Perhaps he thought back to the night when Jesus sat in the house of Simon the Pharisee and the woman poured such expensive perfume on Jesus's feet. She seemed to value his life more than those who were hell-bent on destroying him. She gave her life savings, asking nothing more than the joy of washing his feet. They gave a paltry sum that none of them would miss, to have the life of the Son of God in their vise grip.

Perhaps he wondered if it would be a dark night tonight, for some things are better done in the dark. It had to be done. Someone had to put a stop to this, for Jesus had failed them. After all, where was the revolution that would overthrow the Roman Empire and establish a Jewish kingdom?

JESUS

Had Jesus slept at all the previous night? He knew that he would never sleep another night on this earth. What was on his heart that Thursday morning as he stood up and turned to face the rising sun?

> O safe and happy shelter, O refuge tried and sweet,
> O trysting place where Heaven's love and Heaven's
> justice meet!
> As to the holy patriarch that wondrous dream was given,
> So seems my Savior's cross to me, a ladder up to heaven.[2]

THE PREPARATION

Jesus's disciples asked him where they should prepare to celebrate Passover together that evening. Jesus told them that arrangements had already been made. He told Peter and John to go into the city, and when they saw a man carrying a jar of water, they should follow him. When this man went into his house, they were to ask him where the room was.

It was the custom for women to carry water, so it should not have been difficult to find a man carrying a jar of water. Just as Jesus had said, they found him and he showed them the room where they could get things ready for their meal.

That night, Jesus ate the Passover meal with his closest friends. He told them how much he had looked forward to sharing this meal with them, for he would not celebrate another Passover until the kingdom of God had come. I imagine the disciples talked among themselves, wondering what Jesus was saying. How could they know that they were sharing the final hours with the Son of God, who would take away the sin of the world?

They shared two meals that night. They shared the Passover meal that was known to them, and then Jesus took bread and wine and told them what was about to happen.

A Passover meal had four courses and four cups, plenty of time for Judas to reconsider. But by the time Jesus instituted the new feast and took the bread and the cup, explaining that they represented his body and blood, Judas was already gone. Only those who believed would share that feast.

THE TURNING

There are moments in life when the choices we make have irrevocable consequences.

A pregnant teenager, alone, abandoned by her boyfriend, afraid of her father, signs a consent paper in a clinic and moves forward, no turning back.

A man, sober for twelve years, frustrated by a job that is taking him nowhere, reaches for a glass. He gets into his car and turns the key. He would say later that the car came out of nowhere, but in his cell at night, he knows that he never saw it coming at all.

A passionate, angry man, tired of Roman rule, begins to follow someone who is going somewhere. He can feel the momentum build, but it never produces the results he wants. Yes, the man is gathering a crowd, but they're the wrong people, the nobodies. He feels betrayed, thinking of all the time he's wasted. It's time to cut his losses.

> *There are moments in life when the choices we make have irrevocable consequences.*

THE BETRAYAL

Betrayal feels like grief. It is a wound to the heart. While they ate together that fateful Thursday evening, Jesus gave Judas a moment to reconsider. He said, "'I will dip this bread into the dish. The man I give it to is the man who will turn against me.' So Jesus took a piece of bread, dipped it, and gave it to Judas Iscariot, the son of Simon. As soon as Judas took the bread, Satan entered him. Jesus said to him, 'The thing that you will do—do it quickly'" (John 13:26–27).

Judas took the bread. He could have said no! Instead, he reached out and took it—just as Eve reached out and took the fruit by an act of will. The temptation had no power in itself. Satan looks at us and he knows who we are. He can't make us do anything, but he banks on the fact that we might not know that. Or at least, perhaps we've forgotten. Just like the Wicked Witch of the West, who looked at Dorothy and saw the mark on her forehead, Satan looks at us, and he almost cannot bear to look, for he is looking straight at the image of God.

Satan looks at us and he almost cannot bear to look, for he is looking straight at the image of God.

Once we reach out and "take the bread," we are committed. So Judas chose to leave and hurried out into the cold night air.

This talk of betrayal was new to Peter and John. They had heard Jesus talk about his death but never about betrayal. Peter whispered to John, "Ask him what he means."

John rested his head on Jesus's chest like a little brother and asked, "It's not me, is it, Lord?" Though some versions of Scripture translate this as, "Who is it, Lord?" the Greek is more personal. It suggests that the disciples were bombarding Jesus with emotional responses: "It's not me, is it, Lord? Please tell me it's not me!"

Judas slipped out into the night, and no one but Jesus paid any attention. You see he was the treasurer, the one trusted with the money. What a strange irony. The disciples probably thought that he had to slip out and get something for Jesus. They were right in a way, for he would bring back an execution squad.

Upon that cross of Jesus mine eye at times can see
The very dying form of One Who suffered there for me;
And from my stricken heart with tears two wonders I
    confess;
The wonders of redeeming love and my unworthiness.[3]

A New Feast

Jesus took bread, and he broke it. Then he gave some to his friends. He said to them, "It looks like bread. You'll see it every day, and every time you see it, I want you to remember that this represents my body, which will be broken for you. I have chosen something you see every day because you will need to remember every day for the rest of your lives that I love you and I do this gladly for you.

"So when you fall and you fail and you mess up—because you will, Peter—I have covered you. You will think it's all over when you mess up, but you will be wrong. You see, you can't ever get it right on your own. I know that, and I understand, so I do

"When you are ready to turn again, you will dream a bigger dream. This time it will be my dream for your life, and it will not fail you."

this for you. And when you run out into the darkness tomorrow night because you have failed to do the things you thought you could do, remember that I understand. And when you are ready to turn again, you will dream a bigger dream. This time it will be my dream for your life, and it will not fail you."

Thursday Night

After dinner, Jesus and the disciples sang a hymn and went out to the Mount of Olives and to a garden called Gethsemane. The word *Gethsemane* means "pressed oil." It is the process used to squeeze every drop of oil from an olive, to extract the very life blood of the fruit. Jesus left eight of the disciples at the edge of the garden, and he asked Peter, James, and John to come in deeper with him. Why did he do that? Did he think they could help bear the load? Would they at least weep with him, sweat with him?

He told his three closest friends, "My heart is full of sorrow, to the point of death. Stay here and watch with me" (Matthew 26:38). I can't read these words without weeping. I had to get up three times while writing this chapter and just put my face in my hands and weep. It is tempting as believers to think that because Jesus was fully God as well as fully man, his suffering was somehow easier to bear. He knew it would be over soon. He knew that this gift of suffering would satisfy his Father and save us all.

But he also knew that a moment was coming that no one else in heaven or earth would ever have to face. When he took on the sin of the world, his Father would turn his face away from him and leave him as if in hell.

AND SO IT BEGINS

It wasn't a trial; it was a farce. The religious leaders had no charges that would stick when they dragged him before Caiaphas, the high priest. So the Son of God stood before the man who was God's representative on this earth, and he didn't recognize him.

They brought all sorts of witnesses who had agreed to swear to things that they had never seen, but like most liars, they couldn't get their stories straight. Caiaphas was furious. He would not be humiliated. Everyone was talking and screaming about Jesus. But Jesus himself stood there, silent. His silence condemned them all. They spat on him and slapped him and tore their clothes as heaven watched.

They were getting nowhere at this trial, so they dragged Jesus before Pontius Pilate, the Roman governor.

When Judas heard what was happening, he finally realized what he had done: he had betrayed an innocent man. He tried to return the money, but the priests had no interest in this "blood money." In despair, Judas went out and hanged himself, but even this plan misfired. The rope broke, and as he fell facedown in the field, his blood soaked the earth. The field where he died became known as the Field of Blood.

Pilate recognized that the case against Jesus was a setup and wanted no part of it. But the crowd would not be quiet. It was as if all the demons of hell wore cloaks and sandals that day and yelled, "Crucify him! Crucify him!"

There lies beneath its shadow but on the further side
The darkness of an awful grave that gapes both deep and wide
And there between us stands the cross two arms outstretched
   to save
A watchman set to guard the way from that eternal grave.[4]

IT IS FINISHED

And so they crucified Jesus. It was the worst means of death they could use. No Roman citizen, no matter how heinous an offender, was ever crucified. It usually took two or three days to die in slow, unrelenting agony.

While hanging in anguish on the cross, his life slipping away breath-by-breath, Jesus looked down at the crowd and said to his Father, "Father, forgive them, for they do not know what they are doing" (Luke 23:34 NIV).

From noon until three o'clock, the sky was black. Passover fell on a full moon, so this was not an eclipse of the sun. It was as if all of creation was crying out, *We will not shine, for this is darkness!*

Then Jesus said, "Father, into your hands I commit my spirit" (v. 46 NIV). And he died.

As Jesus took his final breath that day, the veil in the temple was ripped from top to bottom. No man ripped it, for a person would have ripped it from bottom to top. This was heaven's doing. The veil that covered the presence of God was no longer needed. Now all who would come in the name of Jesus would find a place to stand in the presence of God.

It's an unusual crowd for such a holy place. You will find a young girl who signed a consent paper and said good-bye to the child she would never know. There's a man who sits behind bars but stands in the presence of God.

It's a place of broken dreams and new dreams. It's a place of disillusionment and rebirth. It is a place to put away childish dreams and dream a bigger dream—the dream that God has for our lives.

I take, O cross, thy shadow for my abiding place;
I ask no other sunshine than the sunshine of His face;
Content to let the world go by to know no gain or loss,
My sinful self my only shame, my glory all the cross.[5]

13

We're Off to See the Wizard!

CHANGED BY THE JOURNEY

"We shall go to-morrow morning," returned the Scarecrow.
"So now let us get ready for it will be a long journey."
—THE WONDERFUL WIZARD OF OZ

This is My commandment, that you love one another as I have loved
you. Greater love has no one than this, than to lay down one's life for
his friends. You are My friends if you do whatever I command you.
—JOHN 15:12–14 NKJV

His name was Edward. That might seem quite a grand name for a rabbit, but then he was a very fine rabbit. He was made entirely of china apart from his ears and tail, which were fashioned from real fur. He had his own wardrobe of custom-made silk suits and fine leather shoes. Edward's vast selection of hats had holes cut out to accommodate his large rabbit ears. Edward was a gift to ten-year-old Abilene from her grandmother.

Perhaps there had never been a rabbit that was loved as much as Edward. Abilene included him in everything she did. He had his own seat at the dinner table, and if Abilene felt that Edward had missed a part of the conversation, she asked her mother or father to repeat it. Each morning, before she went to school, Abilene sat Edward on a chair facing the window so that he could look out until she returned.

Edward had his own little bed in her room. Every night before she went to sleep, Abilene would say, "I love you, Edward." He accepted her love and thought it appropriate for such a fine rabbit, but he didn't return it. Edward didn't know how to love. He lay each night with his eyes open (as they had been painted that way), and gazed up at the stars waiting for morning.

One day Abilene's grandmother bent down and whispered in Edward's ear, "I am very disappointed in you." Edward was surprised and wondered what she meant. An unusual twist of fate was about to take Edward on a miraculous journey that would change his life and his heart. He would no longer be disappointing.

LEARNING TO LOVE

This is a paraphrase of the beginning of the book *The Miraculous Journey of Edward Tulane,* by Kate DiCamillo.[1] This author has great empathy for her characters and treats their strengths and weaknesses with equal grace and dignity. I love all her books, but my favorite by far is the story of Edward Tulane.

Edward's journey teaches him what it means to love and to lose, to be abandoned and to be found. In his story I hear the echo of T. S. Eliot's profound truth: "We shall not cease from exploration/ and the end of all our exploring/ will be to arrive where we started/ and know the place for the first time."[2]

We're Off to See the Wizard!

I won't spoil the story for you (I think you would love this book!), but that is the great truth that Edward discovers. Life has brought him full circle, only everything has changed because Edward's heart has been changed. Even as he realizes how disappointing life can be, he is awakened to a greater adventure, which is to love and to be loved no matter what the cost.

RETURNING TO OUR FIRST LOVE

Life moves at a fast pace these days, and few of us return in our thirties, forties, or fifties to the places where we began our physical journey on this earth. We may visit if we have family or friends who still live there, or we might return to care for an aging parent. But rarely by choice do we move ourselves back to our roots.

But what about our spiritual journey? Do we ever return to the cross, to the place where our real lives began?

I gave my life to Jesus when I was eleven years old, but I gave him my shame when I was thirty-five. When I started on my Christian journey at eleven, I had a bag full of dreams.

> *I gave my life to Jesus when I was eleven years old, but I gave him my shame when I was thirty-five.*

They were dreams of all the things that I would do for God. When I returned at thirty-five, my bag was empty. I had tried everything that I knew to do to fix my life and to be the "perfect" Christian, but nothing had worked. I came back to where I'd started. I traced my footsteps all the way back to Calvary.

THESE BUTTONS ARE HOPELESS!

When Christian was a little boy, he had a favorite sweater with silver buttons in the shapes of different animals. He asked me to teach him how to button it up by himself. We worked at it for a while, trying to master the manual dexterity it takes to get a small silver pig or puppy through a hole. In no time at all, he was like an old pro.

It is easy to let others into our inner circle when life is going well, but it is life changing to welcome companionship when our dreams have fallen apart.

One morning he came into the kitchen and announced, "Mom, these buttons are hopeless!" He had big tears rolling down his cheeks, which were now red with frustration. I looked at his sweater and saw that he had put the second button in the first hole; so when he got to the bottom of his sweater, he had one hole left but no animal to put in it. He had looked at himself in the mirror and observed that he had a stray cat at the top, so he tried to put the cat from the top through the bottom buttonhole and almost choked himself! I suggested to him that we might need to go right back to the beginning and start again.

Sometimes in our spiritual journey, we have to do that too. We are drawn back to the last place that we know that things were true and aligned correctly. That is always at the cross.

I believe that one of the greatest adventures in life is learning what it means to love and allow others to love us. It is easy to let others into our inner circle when life is going well, but it is life changing to welcome companionship when our dreams have fallen apart. Our broken places show us at our most vulnerable. Naturally, we tend to guard those places most. But, ironically, it is there that we can be most known, received, and helped.

THE VALLEY OF THE SHADOW

As I was sorting through old files the other day, I came across my discharge papers from the psychiatric hospital where I had been a patient for a month in 1992. I hadn't seen them in years, so I sat down and opened the envelope. The first thing that tumbled out was a photograph that had been taken the night I was admitted. I stared at it for a while, remembering that day.

It was an unusually cold September day, but for some reason I was wearing a short-sleeved shirt. I remember sitting in the waiting room, wishing that I had put on something warmer. I felt chilled to the bone. I was very thin and pale. I hadn't eaten much in a few weeks, and I couldn't sleep. When the nurse went through my small suitcase, she asked me why I had only packed summer clothes. I told her that I had no idea.

All that I could remember was that after I had finished the live broadcast of *The 700 Club* that morning, I went home, threw a few things into a suitcase, and began the three-hour drive to the hospital. My boss, Pat Robertson, wanted one of our security staff to drive me, but I couldn't bear the thought of anyone watching me walk through those doors that would lock behind me. I was so ashamed. Everything I had ever dreamed for my life was gone, and I felt as if I was now living in a nightmare.

The nurse took me to my room and started to help me unpack. When she put my belt, pantyhose, makeup, hair dryer, and comb into a separate bag, I asked her why. She told me she had to remove anything I could harm myself with.

That morning I had been on national television hosting my own show; now I was not allowed to hold my own hair dryer.

I didn't sleep much that night. For one thing, I was being checked on every fifteen minutes. That's tough for anyone, but for someone like me who treasures privacy, it was downright traumatic. I felt like an animal in a cage. *How is it possible*, I wondered, *to go from being so in control to being confined in less than twenty-four hours? How is it possible to spend all your life trying to get it right and end up in a place that says you are all wrong?*

A nurse who was going off duty looked into my room one last time on her shift. I was sitting on the floor in the corner, wrapped in a blanket. She came over and sat beside me. She took something out of her pocket and gave it to me. I looked down to see what she had placed in my hand, and it was a small, stuffed lamb. She said, "Don't worry; the Shepherd will find you."

I cried and cried until I had soaked the lamb.

The LORD is my shepherd; I have everything I need.
He lets me rest in green pastures. He leads me to
    calm water.
He gives me new strength. He leads me on paths that
    are right for the good of his name.
Even if I walk through a very dark valley, I will not be
    afraid, because you are with me. (Psalm 23:1–4)

We're Off to See the Wizard!

By God's grace and mercy, we take off on this journey of life with a backpack full of our own dreams. Some will be realized, and some will be disappointed. Some we will continue to pursue, and some we will put down. The fulfillment of some dreams will bring joy, and the shallow rewards of others will break our hearts.

> God is always watching over us and leading us back to his side.

At times our dreams seem to be lost forever, and we can feel as if we are lost too. But we are never lost. I know that to be true. We are never abandoned in the middle of our story. Our Father has known the end from the very beginning.

God is always watching over us and leading us back to his side.

THE COMPANIONSHIP OF BROKENNESS

Inside the locked ward of a psychiatric hospital, I learned that when all social or spiritual positioning is gone, what is left is the level ground at the foot of the cross.

There were about ten others in my group at the hospital. One was a pastor and one a retired missionary. One young girl sat with her wrists bandaged from where she had tried to end her life. Each morning we would repeat this simple prayer, attributed to Reinhold Niebuhr, together: "God grant me the serenity to accept the things I cannot change, courage to change the things I can, and wisdom to know the difference."

There is such liberty in those words. Accepting what we cannot change is a gate out of the past and into today and all that tomorrow will hold. Courage to change what we can says that we are not victims of the whims of others or of the enemy. Only God can grant us the wisdom to know the difference, but he has invited anyone who lacks wisdom to come to him and ask for it (James 1:5).

I could never have been part of a ministry like Women of Faith before my journey to the depths of clinical depression. It would have been far too threatening for me to share a platform with those who stood with unveiled faces. I didn't think that's what anyone wanted from me. But I was wrong. The greatest gift that we can give each other is to tell the truth and, as Max Lucado says, "make a big deal out of God every day of our lives."[3]

A BIGGER DREAM

When we as believers find ourselves having lost our way and come full circle, we are back at the foot of the cross. We stand there with all the other travelers who have lost their way or their hope or their joy.

When all your dreams have been crushed and your heart is broken, you stand in the perfect place for a resurrection.

By the time Edward found his way back to where he started, he had lost his custom-made suits and hats. He had been smashed into many pieces and carefully put back together by a master doll maker. He had none of his stuff, but he had a heart. He had lost what he thought made him beautiful and discovered what matters: to love and be loved.

This is what happened to Peter and the other disciples. This is the story of Dorothy, the Scarecrow, the Tin Woodsman, and the Cowardly Lion. And this is what is offered to you and to me. It is offered not in the far-distant future, but right now.

When all your dreams have been crushed and your heart is broken, you stand in the perfect place for a resurrection.

Sunday Morning

I wonder if every time Peter heard a cock crow again, he was pulled back into that moment. He had sworn on his life that he would never betray Jesus, yet within just a few hours the words, "I never knew him!" tumbled out of his mouth. He was bitterly ashamed. Even when he closed his eyes he could see Jesus looking at him, loving him.

It must have seemed to Peter that life was over. His future looked bleak and disappointing. He would probably return to fishing, but his heart would not be in it. How could he live through another storm and not see Jesus walking across the water toward him? How could he pull in a net full of fish and not remember how Jesus had filled his empty nets one morning? Could he ever visit Mary, Martha, and Lazarus again and look them in the eye? Everyone would know that when Jesus needed him most, he turned and ran.

Friday night turned into Saturday. It was quiet on the Sabbath.

A devout Jew had thirty-nine things he couldn't do on the Sabbath if he wanted to uphold the law. In the strictest interpretation of that law (called the Mishnah) in Jesus's time, the maximum weight one could carry was no more than the weight of a tea-spoon. Tell that to Peter, whose heart was as heavy as lead.

He knew that Mary Magdalene and some of the other women were going early the next day to the tomb with spices to anoint the body of Jesus. But Peter wouldn't go. He couldn't bear to look at the battered and broken body of the dearest friend he had ever known.

Suddenly there was a noise on the stairs. He could hear some-one calling out his name. Something was wrong, but what more could be wrong? Then he saw her. The moment Peter saw Mary's face, he knew. Words and tears tumbled out together.

Peter and John ran to the garden tomb. John was young and fast and got there first, but he couldn't bring himself to go inside. So Peter stepped into the tomb. The clothes that had been wrapped around the body of Christ were lying on the stone slab, but the one that had been around his head was folded neatly and placed apart from the others.

No thief would have taken time to unwrap a body. No grave robber would have folded the linen napkin and placed it carefully on the stone. It lay there as if Jesus had said that not only was his work finished, but he had been in no particular hurry to get out of the tomb, for it held no power over him.

John was standing beside Peter now, and John believed. He wrote it in his own words: "Then the other disciple, who came to the tomb first, went in also; and he saw and believed" (John 20:8 NKJV).

We're Off to See the Wizard!

WHAT NOW?

Peter and John stayed for a while, perhaps wondering what to do next. Then they went home. Mary stayed. She was the first to get there and the last to leave. Jesus had delivered her from a private hell. For years she had lived a tormented life until Jesus cast seven demons out of her.

Mary couldn't bring herself to leave the last place that she knew Jesus had been. As she stood there, she wept so hard that her vision was blurry. She was aware of someone standing behind her and turned around. She didn't know that it was Jesus until he spoke her name.

We read that she clung to Jesus so hard that he had to ask her to release him. It wasn't over. Christ had yet to ascend to his Father.

DREAM A BIGGER DREAM

Mark's Gospel gives us a detail omitted in the other records. It is a wonderful gift to those of us who feel that we have failed Christ and are no longer worthy to be used by him.

When Mary first looked in the tomb, she saw a young man sitting there in a long white robe. He told her not to be afraid. (I am convinced that angels have a sense of humor!) Then he said to her, "You are looking for Jesus from Nazareth, who has been crucified. He has risen from the dead; he is not here. Look, here is the place they laid him. Now go and tell his followers *and Peter*, 'Jesus is going into Galilee ahead of you, and you will see him there as he told you before'" (Mark 16:6–7; emphasis added).

Tell his followers—*and Peter*. I love that! If Mary had rushed back and said that the young man in the tomb told her that the disciples should go to Galilee, would Peter have gone? Would he have wondered if he was welcome after his betrayal?

The angel's specific mention of Peter is a triumphant invitation to those whose dreams lie dead at their feet that it is time to dream again—but this time to dream a bigger dream. Peter was given a dream that was bigger than he was.

THE ROCK

Peter would go on to become the leader of the early church. The one who said he never knew Jesus stood up on the day of Pentecost and declared not only that Jesus was the promised Messiah, but that he had died and been raised from the dead. More than three thousand people gave their lives to Christ that day.

Peter was a changed man. This cowardly apostle who had once denied even knowing Christ lived the rest of his life boldly proclaiming the powerful, saving message of the gospel to everyone who would listen.

WHERE ARE YOU?

I know that God can take the most battered and broken heart and teach it to dream again. As you look at your life today, what are you dreaming for?

You may be dreaming for a husband.

You may be dreaming for a child.

You may be dreaming for a change of career or a new beginning.

All of these are wonderful and valid dreams, and they are dreams that God will heed. But they are not the greatest dream of all. My sincere prayer for you today is that God will give you a fresh vision of his dream for your life.

God has a dream for your life that no other human being on this earth can fulfill. It is time to dismiss the lies of the enemy, who hopes that you never realize who you are.

> *God can take the most battered and broken heart and teach it to dream again.*

PART THREE

There's No Place Like Home

THE DREAM GOD HAS FOR YOUR LIFE

14

An Incredible Journey

DREAMING WITH ONE ANOTHER

*"They will surely tear us to pieces with their sharp claws. But
stand close behind me; and I will fight them as long as I am alive."*
—THE COWARDLY LION, *THE WONDERFUL WIZARD OF OZ*

*Your love must be real. Hate what is evil, and hold on to
what is good. Love each other like brothers and sisters. Give
each other more honor than you want for yourselves.*
—ROMANS 12:9–10

I am a big fan of the Special Olympics. Having spent a summer volunteering in a home for mentally challenged adults, I have
great respect for those with intellectual disabilities; they are much
stronger and braver than most of us "normal" people.

The Special Olympics' commitment to sports training and
competition offers wonderful opportunities to those who are
excluded from many traditional events. It allows them to experience the joy of bringing all you have to the table, of showing
courage and being part of a sporting community.

The first International Special Olympics Summer Games were

held on July 20, 1968. Eunice Kennedy Shriver officially opened the games with these inspiring words: "In ancient Rome, the gladiators went into the arena with these words on their lips: 'Let me win, but if I cannot win, let me be brave in the attempt.' . . . Today, all of you young athletes are in the arena. Many of you will win, but even more important, I know you will be brave and bring credit to your parents and to your country."

The games are always uplifting, but there was one track-and-field event that I will never forget: the 100-meter race. Early in the race, a young athlete tripped and fell. He hit the track hard. The crowd gasped as they watched him tumble and cry out. Then the most amazing thing happened.

The other athletes looked back to see what had happened. When they saw the boy facedown on the track, one by one they turned around and went to his aid. That day, hand in hand, all the runners crossed the finishing line as one. It was quite a sight.

Can you imagine anything like that happening apart from the community that we call mentally challenged? It was one of the most inspiring and humbling events I've ever seen. All I could think as I watched with tears on my cheeks and cheers in my heart was, *That's how we are supposed to be as the body of Christ!*

CHRIST'S PRAYER FOR US

Before Jesus was betrayed and dragged away from his followers, he prayed for them. John's Gospel tells us that he looked down through the years to this very moment and prayed for us too. John records this as the last thing that Jesus did before his betrayal.

In his prayer, Jesus said, "I pray for these followers, but I am also praying for all those who will believe in me because of their teaching. Father, I pray that they can be one. As you are in me and I am in you, I pray that they can also be one in us. Then the world will believe that you sent me" (John 17:20–21).

Immediately after that we read, "When Jesus finished praying, he went with his followers across the Kidron Valley. On the other side there was a garden, and Jesus and his followers went into it" (John 18:1).

I don't wish to belabor the point, but rather to say we can't miss this! Jesus, knowing that he only had hours left to live, prayed for you and for me. He didn't pray that we would be great or build huge buildings. He didn't ask for his Father to make us famous or fulfill all our dreams. He prayed that we would carry his dream. And what was that dream? That we would love one another and that through our love other people would know that God is alive and well. Then people would believe that Jesus had been sent from God to save the world.

Jesus, knowing that he only had hours left to live, prayed for you and for me.

I think Jesus prayed that for two reasons. First, it's almost impossible to love one another, and he knew that we would need God's mighty aid to even attempt it. Second, when we do choose to love by God's grace and mercy, a watching world pays attention.

It was Christ's earnest desire that we would be defined as his people by the way we love one another. Yet I think too often in our culture, Christians are defined by what we stand against.

WHAT IS A CHRISTIAN?

One day I decided to conduct my own little survey in a mall. I got a clipboard and tried to look as if I were there on official business. I wore my most studious-looking glasses, slicked my hair back, and attempted to appear curious but detached.

When I approached my targets, I told them I was conducting a study on religious habits in America. My question was simple: "What is a Christian?" Here are a few of the answers I received:

- "Someone who hates gays"
- "A Republican"
- "Someone who doesn't drink or smoke"
- "A hypocrite"
- "An antiabortionist"

Obviously, these are not the only answers I received. I heard from many believers who said that a Christian is a follower of Christ. But I didn't get a single answer from someone who wasn't a believer that had anything to do with love.

My survey may not have been scientifically accurate, but I don't think its results are very far from how our culture views those who profess to love God.

Many would argue that it is Christians' responsibility to uphold morality in our nation, that we must speak out because the Judeo-Christian values that our nation was founded upon are being embattled and eroded. I agree with that. And I am grateful to those who are gifted and called to be watchmen on the wall.

What I struggle with are those Christians who hate the sinners more than the sin. I was channel surfing one day and stopped on a news channel that was featuring response to a gay-pride parade. On one side of the street were those cheering them on. On the other side were the protesters. Some were peaceful, and others were very vocal. The camera focused in on a small group of Christians who were holding banners that proclaimed their hate.

It broke my heart to look at the faces of those holding the banners. There was no love or compassion there, just unveiled hatred. I can't understand how a child of God could get off his or her knees in prayer and then move to that place of hatred.

That is not how Jesus told us to live. It will never change our world or compel anyone to the foot of the

Jesus prayed that we would love one another in the family of God, and that love would be a sign to the world.

cross. But it may well chase them away. If I had been there, I would have set up a lemonade stand and prayed for opportunities to talk about a deeper thirst.

Not only are Christians perceived to be critical and unaccepting of those outside our doors, but we have a hard time loving those in the pew behind us. Jesus prayed that we would love one another in the family of God, and that love would be a sign to the world.

Why is it so hard to love? I think one reason we struggle to love as Christ commanded is that we judge one another without really knowing one another. We view other believers through our own cultural or denominational perspective and then make quick decisions based on first impressions. We often cloak our judgment in spiritual language and present it as "discernment." But biblical discernment is a spiritual gift, not a personal prejudice.

Judgment Instead of Grace

When I went to seminary as a nineteen-year-old, I felt as if I had been given a little piece of heaven on earth. As I boarded the train in Glasgow that day for the seven-hour trip to London, I was so excited. Not only would I be living in a city that is bursting at the seams with great music and art and theater, but I would spend the next few years studying with other believers.

In high school, I was one of only a handful of students who even went to church. So the idea of being part of a community of Christ's followers was captivating.

Then I got there.

The ratio of male to female students was two male students for every one female. This seemed like a grand idea to me. I was sure that I would be Mrs. Somebody in no time at all. Most of the men were studying for the pastorate. The women were either training to be teachers or missionaries.

I wasn't quite sure what I was training for. I had an idea that God might want me in India, but I was praying that I wouldn't have to go there alone! I didn't think it would be appropriate to put "minister's wife—minister not yet found" on the professional goal part of my application form, so I put "youth evangelist/missionary."

It was obvious to me that my style was different from most of the other girls. They favored long skirts and knitted sweaters, whereas I liked jeans and boots and leather jackets. I didn't think that would matter a bit and was looking forward to making new friends.

One day I was crossing the courtyard to the library when I saw a small group of girls sitting in a circle praying. I decided to join them. I was just in time to hear one girl ask God to give more wisdom and modesty to "the hussy in the red leather boots." Yes, that was me.

I was so embarrassed. I got up quickly to try and get away before they realized I was there, but in my haste I dropped my books. It was a very awkward moment for all. That night, I cried myself to sleep. I felt rejected and judged based on nothing more than my very cool boots.

But I've done it too—only in other ways.

Some years ago, a friend of mine confessed to me that she was gay. She was married, and she and her husband were in counseling together. She asked me for my prayers. When she needed me most, I backed away. In my selfishness, I thought that she was making a pass at me. (Years later, when I had asked her to forgive me and we were close again, she teasingly told me that I was not her type!)

My fear held me back from being the fragrance of Christ to one who was hurting. She needed the support of a sister to help her cross the finishing line, but I cared more about my own image or how her struggle would affect me.

GOD USES PAIN AS A BRIDGE

One of the most profound experiences for me over the last few years has been to see the way God uses pain as a bridge to

One of the most profound experiences for me over the last few years has been to see the way God uses pain as a bridge to connect women.

connect women. When we struggle with anything that is shame-based, it can isolate us and cut us off from what we need most: companionship and comfort.

Patsy Clairmont jokes from the Women of Faith conference stage about how hard it can be for women to cheer each other on. "You hear that a friend has been promoted at work or someone else in the choir gets the solo and you say, 'I'm so happy for you,' while privately you're thinking, *She makes me sick!*"

Jealousy can eat at our hearts like a foul cancer. It distracts us from experiencing the dream that God has for each of us. The root of jealousy is fear: fear that someone else is more loved or more accepted than we are.

FOR GOD'S SAKE

The apostle Paul addressed this issue briefly in his letter to the church at Philippi. We looked earlier at the beginnings of the Philippian church, where a small group of women met by the water to worship. Lydia and her family gave their lives to Christ, and many other women followed. The church began to grow, but trouble was brewing: two of the prominent women in the church, Euodia and Syntyche, could not get along.

Not much is written about the dispute, but the fact that Paul felt compelled to include it in his letter to the church is significant. He says, "I implore Euodia and I implore Syntyche to be of the same mind in the Lord" (Philippians 4:2 NKJV). I can't imagine how humiliating it would be to show up in such a significant letter from Paul to the entire church family in Philippi.

The women in Philippi loved and honored Paul. It is thought most likely that Euodia and Syntyche were of the same class of women as Lydia, women who underwrote much of Paul's work for the gospel. Part of his letter is his deep gratitude for all they have done for him. Now he writes from prison and begs these two women to put their differences aside for the sake of the kingdom.

As I read the letter, I wondered why Paul didn't write a separate note just to the women in question. Was Paul merely putting two difficult women in their places? Did he intend to embarrass them into behaving? I don't think so at all. The note in the book of Philippians is there because God wanted it there. Many of Paul's letters contained instruction to a fledgling church on how to handle problems among believers.

Rather than dishonoring these two women, Paul was indicating how crucial these women were to the work of the Lord. He goes on to say, "And I urge you also, true companion, help these women who labored with me in the gospel" (v. 3 NKJV). The Greek word used here for "labored" is a strong one. It calls up the picture of gladiators fighting side by side for victory. Paul is urging the believers in Philippi to put aside their differences, which are small in light of the gospel of Christ.

The tone of Paul's letter to the church in Philippi shows how much these women have blessed and encouraged him. As a brother he is urging them, not knowing how long he has left on this earth, to rise above whatever is tearing them apart. That is true love.

We all get caught up in petty differences that can get blown out of proportion. Sometimes we are so stubborn that we back ourselves into a corner and can't get out. Paul, in love, is saying in essence, "Come on, girls; you are better than this. Don't let the enemy spoil what God wants to do here." It's a reminder that we often need.

We will never be able to get along with one another on our own. But the great news is that we aren't asked to do it on our own. It is the life and love of Christ himself that gives us strength to do the things that are impossible for us, left to our own abilities.

Paul rejoices in Christ as the source of our strength:

"Does your life in Christ give you strength? Does his love comfort you? Do we share together in the spirit? Do you have mercy and kindness? If so, make me very happy by having the same thoughts, sharing the same love, and having one mind and purpose. When you do things, do not let selfishness or pride be your guide. Instead, be humble and give more honor to others than to yourselves. Do not be interested only in your own life, but be interested in the lives of others." (Philippians 2:1–4)

BUT HOW, LORD?

How in the world are we going to be able to carry out this daunting spiritual mandate to love one another? In a world where our circumstances and our relationships change every day, it helps to take stock of what we know for sure. What can we anchor our lives to that will not change, no matter what is going on around us? An anchor that will help us demonstrate the kind of love and humility that Paul is talking about.

As I prayed to God and asked these questions, God's answer to my heart was twofold:

1. *I love you unconditionally.*
2. *I am in control.*

As I began to ask God to help me live in the truth of these two things, I can honestly say my life radically changed.

Think about this for your own life. Stop for a moment and just let this truth enfold you:

God loves me.
God knows everything about me, and he loves me.
I did nothing to earn God's love, and I cannot lose it.

That is the absolute truth. God loves you passionately, right now. He knows everything about you, your hopes and fears, your dreams and disappointments. There is nothing you can do today or tomorrow to change his love for you.

Not only that, but he is in control. You don't have to fight to make things happen. You don't have to feel threatened when God blesses someone else's life; you can celebrate it! You won't miss a thing that God has for you. Because God is omniscient (all-knowing), omnipotent (all-powerful), and omnipresent (with us all at all times), we can rest.

LOVING AND POWERFUL

If God were loving but not in control, we would be justified in feeling that life is too unpredictable. We would then be like waves tossed on the ocean. God would want to help us but would not be able to.

If God, on the other hand, were sovereign but not loving, we could understandably live in fear. He might turn on us at any moment. He is in control, but what does he think of us?

Here's the best news in the world: God is good and powerful, and he is watching over you, holding your dreams with care.

If you can begin to believe that—not just in your head but all the way down to your heart—it will change your life. You can't lose. You may have to surrender some smaller dreams along the way, but God promises that no one who puts her trust in him will ever be put to shame.

Here's the best news in the world: God is good and powerful, and he is watching over you, holding your dreams with care.

FREE TO LOVE

When the truth of God's love is tucked into our lives, we are free to love, free to give, free to dance as if no one is watching. It makes us the ideal traveling companions.

When I look at the message presented in *The Wonderful Wizard of Oz*, the thing that I find most charming about all the characters is their humility:

- The Tin Woodsman is especially careful not to hurt anyone because he doesn't have a heart to guide him.
- The Scarecrow thinks of himself as a fool, yet time after time he is the one who solves their problems.
- The Cowardly Lion judges himself harshly but is prepared to fight to the death to defend his friends.
- And even though everyone in Oz treated Dorothy as a very special, gifted person, she knew that she was just a little girl from Kansas.
- Even the great Oz himself had the courage to say that he was not a bad man, just a bad wizard.

Because of their humility, these friends served one another. Just like the Olympic runners that day, they were determined to cross the finish line *together*.

FOOT WASHING FOR BEGINNERS

On the night he was betrayed, Jesus gave his friends a lesson on what true servant leadership looks like. "Taking a towel, he wrapped it around his waist. Then he poured water into a bowl and began to wash the followers' feet, drying them with the towel that was wrapped around him" (John 13:4–5).

Peter was shocked by this and wanted to refuse. To a big, burly fisherman like Peter, it seemed demeaning that Jesus would be on his hands and knees washing off the grime of the dusty streets. Jesus told Peter that if he refused, he was not one of his people. That was not what Peter intended at all. He responded boldly, "Lord, then wash not only my feet, but wash my hands and my head, too!" (John 13:9).

Jesus responded that when a person has had a bath, he only needs his feet washed. The literal and cultural interpretation of that is clear. According to first-century social customs, once a person has bathed, he needed only to wash his feet before he ate; the rest of him was clean.

But there is a deeper meaning here, pointing to what Christ was about to do. I hope this will be an encouragement to those of you who find it hard to forgive yourself for past sins. Jesus was saying that once a believer has been washed by his blood and the Word of God, all the believer needs to take care of is the "dust" of the day. The rest is settled. He proclaims, "You are already clean because of the word which I have spoken to you" (John 15:3 NKJV).

> *How would it transform our hearts, our homes, and our churches if we all took a course in feet washing?*

Again in the book of Titus, we are told, "When the kindness and the love of God our Savior toward man appeared, not by works of righteousness which we have done, but according to His mercy He saved us, through the washing of regeneration and renewing of the Holy Spirit . . ." (3:4–6 NKJV).

Once you have asked God to forgive your sins, they are gone—

you don't have to ever mention them again. It doesn't matter what the sin was; it is covered by the blood of the Lamb.

So how should we love one another? How would it transform our hearts, our homes, and our churches if we all took a course in feet washing? When Jesus finished washing the disciples' feet, he sat down with them again and told them to do this for one another.

If we're honest, most of us would probably respond to Jesus's call to wash one another's feet with, *Well, I would do it for* her *(she's pretty nice), but not for* her *(she thinks she's better than us). She would never do that for me.* If that's what you've been thinking, great! Then be like Jesus and start with the one who would never do it for you. Part of God's dream for your life is to set you free from the world and its way of thinking.

Dare to be different. Dare to believe that because you are loved unconditionally every day, you can choose to love like that too. Dare to dream that because God is in control, you can genuinely want more honor for those around you than you do for yourself. With all of heaven watching, dare to dream like Jesus!

15

Suddenly, the Wind Changed

DREAMING AT THE CROSSROADS

*Instantly she was whirling through the air, so swiftly that
all she could see or feel was the wind whistling past her ears.*

—THE WONDERFUL WIZARD OF OZ

*I look up to the hills, but where does my help come from? My help comes
from the LORD, who made heaven and earth. He will not let you be defeated.
He who guards you never sleeps. He who guards Israel never rests or sleeps.
The LORD guards you. The LORD is the shade that protects you from the sun.
The sun cannot hurt you during the day, and the moon cannot hurt you at
night. The LORD will protect you from all dangers; he will guard your life.
The LORD will guard you as you come and go, both now and forever.*

—PSALM 121

One of my most vivid memories from childhood is of my mother doing a final quick check of the house before she went anywhere. She never knew who she might bump into in town and want to invite home for tea. It seemed to me, until recently, that this way of life had disappeared into the same cosmic vat that absorbed Cabbage Patch dolls and disco music.

Then we moved to Frisco, Texas! Now my Women of Faith

friends Mary Graham, Luci Swindoll, Marilyn Meberg, Nicole Johnson, and Patsy Clairmont all live within four miles of our home. Most weeks we plan to do things together, but we also still bump into each other at the mall, Starbucks, or the movie theater. We go to the same dentist and the same doctors, and we even use the same pest-control guy, whom we call Mike, the Highly-Thought-Of Bug Man.

One of the joys of living so close is that we can bounce ideas off one another. One morning, during the writing of this book, Barry and I sat down with some friends from Women of Faith to discuss next year's preconference plans. As we prayed and talked about our audience and the letters we receive, several things became clear to us:

Many women . . .
- have given up on their dreams;
- feel as if they have no time to dream;
- are too afraid to dream;
- ask, "Who am I to dream?";
- ask, "Is it self-indulgent to dream?";
- wonder if it's even Christian to dream.

But the most overwhelming conviction that seems to keep many women caged is this: "I believe that I took a wrong turn somewhere in life, and I lost my dream. I will never find the right road again."

Have you ever felt that way? Do you question whether or not God sees you and knows where you live? It's easy to believe that God knows where Billy Graham lives, but what about where you live?

Many of us can identify with the lyrics of the popular song by Casting Crowns, "Who Am I":

Who am I, that the Lord of all the earth would care to know
my name
Would care to feel my hurt
Who am I, that the Bright and Morning Star would choose to
light the way
For my ever-wandering heart[1]

Sometimes we have to get really lost to understand that God never loses track of us for a moment.

THE JOURNEY

When I was eleven years old, I made the huge decision to become a Christian. My leap of faith was precipitated by a gospel concert by The Heralds, held in the very same movie theater where I often lost myself in dreams on the silver screen. I don't remember much about the actual concert. I do remember that the trombone player wore bright red pants, which was quite a statement in our small conservative community, so I liked him immediately.

Then the evangelist who closed the evening made a simple declaration

> It's easy to believe that God knows where Billy Graham lives, but what about where you live?

that changed my life: "God has no grandchildren, only sons and daughters." It suddenly became clear to me that although my brother, sister, and I accompanied my mother to church as often as it was open, I stood outside the kingdom of God. I listened to our

183

Then the evangelist who closed the evening made a simple declaration that changed my life: "God has no grandchildren, only sons and daughters."

minister, sang the hymns, and learned my memory verses, but I had never made a personal choice to begin a journey with God. I was just trotting along beside my mom, trusting that she knew where she was going.

That night I knelt by my bed, and my mom led me in a simple prayer. I told God that I was deeply sorry for being a sinner. I asked God to forgive me and to give me a new heart and a new beginning.

"So is that it, Mom?" I asked after I prayed. "Am I a Christian now?"

"You are indeed," she said with tears running down her cheeks. "The Bible says, 'Therefore, if anyone is in Christ, he is a new creation; the old has gone, the new has come!'" (2 Corinthians 5:17 NIV).

Is That It?

And so I began my journey. It would take me over terrain that would be lush and exquisite as well as paths that have been rough and confusing. I was just a child, but the question I asked my mother was a serious one.

In essence, I was asking, "Is that it? Having prayed that prayer, will everything make sense to me now? Will life fall into place and the road ahead be clear? Will I understand what is going on inside of me and outside of me? Am I free now? Am I an insider who finally understands the secret of life?"

If only becoming a Christian were like becoming twelve. One day you are eleven, and the next you are twelve. When you wake up on that eventful morning, there is nothing special for you to do other than be grateful for your birthday gifts. You don't have to try to *be* twelve; you just are. You don't have to work at *being* twelve; it just happens. In my experience, being a Christian is not quite that clear-cut. Many of us feel lost on our journey.

The truth is that we all feel a little lost in this world. The old gospel hymn "This world is not my home; I'm just a passin' through" strikes a strong chord in my spirit these days. As daughters of Eve, we all experience the sense of loss that she tasted.

In *Paradise Lost*, John Milton expressed it this way:

Her rash hand in evil hour
Forth reaching to the fruit, she pluck'd, she ate:
Earth felt the wound, and Nature from her seat
Sighing, through all her Works gave signs of woe,
That all was lost.[2]

WHAT IF I CHOOSE THE WRONG PATH?

One of the great fears that I had as a young believer was, "What if I miss God's will for my life? What if my great call to be a missionary in China was delivered from the pulpit while I was in the bathroom?"

As you look at your life today, do you ever think to yourself, *Is this it?*

I turned fifty in the summer of 2006, and as I look back over

What if I miss God's will for my life? What if my great call to be a missionary in China was delivered from the pulpit while I was in the bathroom?

the years, I realize that the greatest gift I've received is the absolute conviction that I am not lost, have never been lost, and will never be lost to God. He is on the throne, and he is God all the time. As the psalmist wrote, "He who guards you never sleeps" (Psalm 121:3).

But truth be told, even though I believe these words of Scripture, at times I still feel adrift in this world. I sense that from many of the women I meet.

WE ARE NOT LOST TO GOD

Being lost is something Jesus directly addresses in Luke's Gospel. The story of the two brothers in Christ's parable of the prodigal son reflects that it is just as easy to feel lost in religion as it is in self-indulgent hedonism.

This story is the last of three illustrations that Jesus gives in Luke 15 concerning loss: the lost sheep, the lost coin, and the lost son. Each story is a compelling apologetic for the outrageous love of God.

In the first, the shepherd leaves ninety-nine sheep on the hillside and goes off in search of one that has lost its way. I grew up in a farming community, and it is an accepted fact that sheep are dumb. They tend to stick together, but if one gets lost and falls down, it cannot get back up by itself—and its fellow sheep can't help. The shepherd, knowing that, leaves everything behind to rescue the one who went to the restroom when the missionary was talking.

In the second, a woman who had ten coins loses one. She stops everything and turns the house upside down until she finds it. The message is clear: God will do whatever it takes to find the lost one, no matter how long it takes.

The third story is the most fleshed out. Jesus said, "A man had two sons. The younger son said to his father, 'Give me my share of the property.' So the father divided the property between his two sons. Then the younger son gathered up all that was his and traveled far away to another country. There he wasted his money in foolish living. After he had spent everything . . . the son left and went to his father. while the son was still a long way off, his father saw him and felt sorry for his son. So the father ran to him and hugged and kissed him" (Luke 15:11–14, 20).

This parable is often used as an encouragement to parents when a child has wandered away from God. That part of the story is clear: no matter how far away you go or how low you fall, God is waiting for you with open arms.

But it is easy to miss an important part of the story. As the story reaches its climax, we can discern that the "good son" who stayed home feels lost in a more profound way.

COME JOIN THE PARTY

The older son was returning from a hard day's work in the field. As he got closer to the house, he could tell that there was a party going on. He asked one of the servants what was happening, and the servant informed him that his little brother had come home and his father was hosting a celebration. The older brother was furious and refused to come in.

When his dad came out to find him, the older brother said, "I have served you like a slave for many years and have always obeyed your commands. But you never gave me even a young goat to have at a feast with my friends. But your other son, who wasted all your money on prostitutes, comes home, and you kill the fat calf for him!" (Luke 15:29–30).

The older brother was furious that he had kept all the rules, yet it was his wastrel of a brother who was getting a party. It seemed so unfair to him. It was as if bad behavior was being rewarded.

This story would be shocking to an audience of Jews, who placed so much emphasis on following all the rules.

The Father looks down at each of us, and when he sees us covered by the blood of his Son, we are welcomed.

Part of the offense of the gospel is that God invites anyone to the foot of the cross. He invites those who are lost in drug abuse or alcohol or meaningless sexual relationships. He invites the adulterer, the gambler, and the criminal. He invites those who have sinned in the ways that are the most obvious. He welcomes all who are lost. And then he throws them a party.

That is grace: the unmerited favor of God. It doesn't sit well with those of us who carry an internal scale to weigh the weight of sin. The older brother felt that all the good he had done should matter. I have real sympathy for him. I've felt that way too. But grace will have none of it.

If we think back to the angel of death passing over Egypt that terrible night, the only thing he looked for was the blood on the doorpost. It is the same with you and me. The Father looks down at each of us, and when he sees us covered by the blood of his Son, we are welcomed.

Everyone's Invited

One of the most effective evangelists of the nineteenth century was "Uncle" John Vassar. His family owned a brewery in New York, and everyone assumed that he would follow in his father's footsteps. But John believed that God had called him to distribute Bibles and tracts, so he left the brewery and took to the road.

On one such trip he met a woman who was concerned about her husband. The man was not a Christian and was antagonistic to her attempts to share her faith. John gave her a Bible and suggested that she give it to her husband. When her husband saw what she had put in his hands, he was furious. He took the Bible outside and chopped it in two with an ax. Telling his wife that half of everything they owned was hers, he gave her one part and threw the other in the shed.

Months later, as he sat in the shed on a cold winter's day, he came across his part of the Bible. As he thumbed through the pages, he came to the story of the prodigal son. He was captivated by the story and was anxious to know how it ended. Unfortunately, the ending was in his wife's half. After a fruitless

No matter where you have lost your way, your Father has never lost track of you.

search, he had to humble himself and ask her where it was. As he read the conclusion of the story, he saw himself and surrendered his life to a waiting Father.

Fortunately, God invites to himself those who have messed up. He also invites the self-righteous, the judgmental, and the hypocritical. He invites those whose sins are kept a secret. He invites the bitter, the angry, and the disappointed. He doesn't invite us because he's impressed by our accomplishments or because he admires our self-direction. He invites us solely because he loves us. And when we come to him, he makes us his daughters. His princesses. We have the power we need because we know who our Father is.

SOMEONE TO WATCH OVER ME

I wish I could sit down with you right now and look you straight in the eyes and tell you how much God loves you. You might feel as if you are on the wrong road, but you aren't. God is right there. No matter where you have lost your way, your Father has never lost track of you.

I don't know where you are in your journey today. What I do know is that God loves you and has never taken his eyes off you. I also know that one of the greatest gifts to us in this life is the companionship of others so that we might finish the journey together.

16

You've Had the Power All Along

DREAMING WITH OUR FATHER

"Your Silver Shoes will carry you over the desert," replied Glinda.
"If you had known their power you could have gone back to
your Aunt Em the very first day you came to this country."

—THE WONDERFUL WIZARD OF OZ

Is this not the fast that I have chosen: to loose the bonds of wickedness, to
undo the heavy burdens, to let the oppressed go free, and that you break every
yoke? . . . Then your light shall break forth like the morning, your healing
shall spring forth speedily, and your righteousness shall go before you; the
glory of the Lord shall be your rear guard. Then you shall call, and the LORD
will answer.

—ISAIAH 58:6, 8–9 NKJV

On February 2, 2006, Bono, lead singer of U2, stood at the podium in the ballroom of the Washington Hilton and began to talk. It was not his usual crowd. There were no screaming fans or disco balls in the shape of a giant lemon. It was the National Prayer Breakfast, and he was the keynote speaker. President Bush and First Lady Laura Bush listened as this rock star shared his heart.

"It's time to stop asking God to bless what you're doing," Bono said. "Get involved with what God is doing, because it's already blessed."

THE BEGINNING OF A DREAM

It all began with a fourteen-year-old boy, Larry Mullen, posting a note on his school notice board in Dublin, Ireland. He was looking for people to join him in forming a band. Seven people showed up for the audition, which was held in his mother's kitchen. Two of them dropped out, and the five remaining boys became the band. For the first week they were called The Larry Mullen Band, but the rest of the band didn't like that, so they became Feedback.

A year and a half later, they won a talent competition in Limerick, Ireland, and changed their name to U2. The rest, as they say, is rock-and-roll history. U2 is now considered by many to be the best rock group in the world. They have sold more than 50 million albums in America and 150 million worldwide.

I don't imagine that as a young teenager, Paul Hewson (Bono's given name) ever saw himself standing up talking to an American audience with the president just four seats away. He didn't see himself as a speaker at all; he was a musician.

Bono's religious upbringing was confusing at best. His father was Roman Catholic and his mother Protestant in a country torn apart by religious hatred. But God saw this young boy with a hot head and a passionate heart and planted a dream in Bono's heart to make a difference in the world. Bono just wasn't sure how that would happen.

You've Had the Power All Along

In July 1985, the Live Aid concert in London was seen by more than one billion people worldwide. This concert raised money for famine relief in Ethiopia. U2 was asked to perform. It was a great chance for the band to be introduced to a much wider audience. They had planned carefully what songs they would sing, but during a rendition of their song "Bad," Bono got caught up in the moment. He vaulted off the stage and began dancing with a girl in the audience. The song went on for thirteen minutes and cancelled out the rest of their set.

The rest of the band was furious with him and suggested he should leave the group. Instead, he took some time out to do some soul searching. When he returned, the group continued to make records and tour, and God continued unfolding a dream in Bono's heart.

NOT A MAN OF THE CLOTH
UNLESS YOU COUNT LEATHER

So Bono stood in front of the crowd at the National Prayer Breakfast as it was being carried live on television across America, and he shared this passage from Isaiah that he knew by heart: "Then your light shall break forth like the morning, your healing shall spring forth speedily, and your righteousness shall go before you; the glory of the LORD shall be your rear guard" (58:8 NKJV).

He told President Bush and the rest of the audience that this seemed to be the best deal going: do the things that God cares about, and he's got your back. Bono didn't get to that place of spiritual maturity or influence overnight. He dreamed many dreams along the way, and then he discovered the dream that God had for his life.

ARE YOU READY?

Are you ready to discover God's dream for your life and take off flying like the wind?

Think back on who you were as a little girl. What were the things that you loved to do more than anything else? What were the moments that made you feel alive, as if this were what you were placed on this earth to do? I joke with Christian that throughout my elementary school years, I was punished for talking in class. Now it is my life.

Are you ready to discover God's dream for your life and take off flying like the wind?

What were the things about you that stood out? Did you line up your dolls and teach them or make things with your hands? Could you run faster than anyone in your class? I love the line from the movie *Chariots of Fire*, when the lead character, Eric Liddell says, "I believe God made me for a purpose, but he also made me fast. And when I run, I feel his pleasure."[1]

That is a profoundly spiritual statement. We think that ministry or worship is something that only happens on Sunday mornings or Wednesday nights. But God asks us to bring everything we have to the table and offer it as an act of worship every day.

You've Had the Power All Along

OUR LEGACY AS DAUGHTERS OF EVE

I don't know if you have ever had the joy of visiting the Sistine Chapel in Rome. I have not seen it in person, but I have studied pictures of Michelangelo's breathtaking paintings on the ceiling of the chapel. He was asked to paint in a genre that was not familiar to him: fresco painting. In this method, the artist paints in pigment with water onto fresh or wet plaster or limestone. The painting dries at the same time as the wall and so becomes part of the structure.

The ceiling that Michelangelo painted is magnificent. He worked on it for four years. There are more than three hundred biblical characters represented, and two of the pictures are of Eve.

When Michelangelo painted Eve, he put the picture of her fall and banishment from the Garden of Eden to one side of the center. His magnum opus, the center point of the ceiling, is Eve's creation from Adam's side.

Art historians say that the placement of Michelangelo's paintings was driven by his theology. By placing Eve's creation right in the middle of his work, he left us with a picture of how God always intended us to be and how, through Christ, we will be again one day. Eve was intended to be the perfect instrument for God's plan. When she failed, God still chose to use her. Yes, she fell and fell hard, but by God's grace and mercy she was still central to his divine plan.

In the Garden of Eden, God gave Adam and Eve a mandate to be fruitful and multiply, to rule over the earth as God's image bearers (Genesis 1:28). As daughters of Eve, we are called to be the best mothers and sisters and friends that we can be. Whether we sit in an office on Wall Street or fold three loads of laundry a day after packing lunch boxes, we are called to do it as daughters of the King. By God's grace, we do everything as if God is right there watching—because he is.

Carolyn Custis James, in her fabulous book *Lost Women of the Bible*, writes that our call is not only a call to reproduce children, but it is "the call to reproduce spiritually by multiplying worshippers of the living God and to extend God's gracious rule over every inch of this planet."[2]

ONE LIFE

Each one of us is given only one life. Your days on earth are not a dress rehearsal so that you can come back and try again. Every life counts. Your life counts.

> *Your days on earth are not a dress rehearsal so that you can come back and try again. Every life counts. Your life counts.*

You may be reading this and thinking, *That's easy for you to say as you travel all over the country to speak to thousands of women while dressed in fine suits and tripping over your four-inch heels. But I've got three kids, a bad back, and a husband who snores!*

Well, first of all, bless your heart! I will say a little prayer for you. Second, that's irrelevant. Your life as it is today matters to God. Why else would he have assigned angels to watch over you at all times? "For He shall give His angels charge over you, to keep you in all your ways. In their hands they shall bear you up, lest you dash your foot against a stone" (Psalm 91:11–12 NKJV).

Heaven is watching us to see what we will do with the life we have been given.

Perhaps as you think about this, you are convinced that you have blown your chance. You know with-

Heaven is watching us to see what we will do with the life we have been given.

out a shadow of a doubt that God called you to do something with your life, but you messed up, so it's too late. Think again.

IT'S NEVER TOO LATE

God used Queen Esther from the Old Testament at a critical time in Israel's history, but only after she had made some very strange choices.

Esther was one of the children of Israel carried into captivity with the prophet Jeremiah about 600 BC. She lived with her family in Susa, a city somewhere to the southwest in Persia (modern-day Iran). In 539 BC, Jews were allowed to return to Israel, but for whatever reason, Esther's family chose to stay in Persia.

After her parents died, Esther was raised by her cousin Mordecai. He adored young Esther, whose life was about to collide with Xerxes, the king of Persia.

Xerxes was the most powerful man in the world at that time. He was a man of limitless extravagance. We read in the book of Esther that he threw a big party that went on for about six months. It was a ridiculously lavish affair for all the noblemen in the land. Then he held a seven-day feast in the grounds of his palace for every man in his kingdom, great or insignificant.

On the seventh day, when he was extremely drunk, Xerxes ordered seven men to tell his wife, Queen Vashti, to come out and parade in her finest for all the men to see. She refused.

The king now had a problem. He had to save face in front of all his men, so he banished the queen from the palace. Then the king sent out a proclamation that every wife should obey her husband in every detail. (Yikes!)

COME ON DOWN! YOU'RE THE
NEXT QUEEN OF PERSIA!

The king began to miss his wife, so his advisers said he should round up all the young virgins in the land and choose a new queen. Esther was among the young girls taken to the palace. Mordecai told her not to reveal that she was a Jew. By law, the king had to marry a virgin from one of the seven great Persian families.

Hegai, the caretaker of the young girls, was impressed with Esther and took her to see the king. He thought she was beautiful, so he put her into the getting-ready-to-spend-the-night-with-the-king program. This took twelve months! She was instructed to spend six months soaking in oil and six months being perfumed and pampered. (Clearly, I am in the wrong job!)

At the end of that time, beautified and truly pickled, she spent the night with the king. He was so pleased with her that he made her Queen Esther. For the next five years, this Jewish bride did everything she could to please her husband.

POOR CHOICES?

I find it interesting that although many Bible commentators are very critical of Rahab the prostitute before she came to faith, they don't say much about Esther other than that she saved her people. I'm sure it is hard for me to understand the pressure that Esther faced, but it seems as if she forgot who she was.

Her name wasn't Esther. Her Jewish name was Hadassah, which had been changed to protect her identity. She auditioned for the position of queen by having sex with a man who wasn't her husband and who was a pagan.

While all this was happening in Persia, back in her homeland the prophet Ezra was calling God's people to repent for marrying outside their race. He said, "We were slaves. Yet our God did not forsake us in our bondage; but He extended mercy to us in the sight of the kings of Persia, to revive us, to repair the house of our God, to rebuild its ruins, and to give us a wall in Judah and Jerusalem. . . . Now therefore, do not give your daughters as wives for their sons, nor take their daughters to your sons; and never seek their peace or prosperity. . . . Should we again break Your commandments, and join in marriage with the people committing these abominations?" (Ezra 9:9, 12, 14 NKJV).

SIGN OF THE TIMES

I think that what happened to Esther could be compared to what happens to a lot of kids when they go off to college. Imagine a young girl raised in a good Christian home. She is surrounded by positive input from her family, her friends, and her church community. Then for the first time in her life, she is away from home and thrust into a community where people don't hold the same values. It is easy to get caught up in the prevailing atmosphere.

What I love about Esther's story is that when God sent her a wake-up call, she responded immediately.

IT IS NEVER TOO LATE
TO REMEMBER WHO YOU ARE

Mordecai's archrival was Haman. He hated the Jews and was determined to see every Jew in the Persian Empire wiped out. And as King Xerxes' second in command, Haman had the power to do it. He told the king that a certain group of foreigners were causing trouble and he would like to take care of them. With careless disregard, the king signed the decree that stated that on a certain day, all the Jews in Persia should be put to death.

When Mordecai discovered what was planned, he told Esther that she had to go to the king and plead with him to intervene. Esther was horrified. The king hadn't called for her in a month, and to go into his chambers without being summoned meant almost certain death.

Mordecai showed little pity for her condition. He told her that God would not spare her if she turned her back on all her people. Esther had to choose now where she would stand. Believing in the sovereignty of God, her cousin said to her, "Who knows, you may have been chosen queen for just such a time as this" (Esther 4:14).

This is your moment, Esther—take it now.

You've Had the Power All Along

My Life Is in Your Hands

All the Jewish people fasted and prayed for three days. Esther dressed in her finest clothes and began the long walk to stand in the inner court across from the king's house. When she looked up, she could see him on his throne, and she knew that her life could be over in a moment.

By God's grace, the king received Esther and asked what she wanted. She told him that she wanted to host a banquet for the king and Haman.

After they were seated and enjoying the meal, Xerxes offered Esther half of his kingdom. In response, she asked simply for her life and the life of her people. When he asked who had threatened her, she pointed to Haman. As punishment, Haman was hung on the very gallows that he had constructed to hang Mordecai, and the lives of all the Jewish people were spared.

God Has a Big Dream for Your Life!

We get funny ideas of what it looks like to be a godly woman. We think that God's dream for our lives would have us running around like spiritual versions of Wonder Woman:

"Today, I will learn three chapters of the New Testament while knitting blankets for the poor. Then after breakfast, I will lead two neighbors to Christ. One will become a missionary in China, while the other will get hit by a Mack truck before reaching the supermarket, therefore bypassing the produce aisle and going straight to heaven!

"After lunch, I will visit my mother-in-law in the nursing home. I will laugh at her good-humored-yet-hurtful comments about the color of my hair and then lead all the residents in a time of worship. After supper, my son and I will build a life-size working model of Mount Vesuvius erupting for his science project.

"Tonight, I will give my husband his slippers, which I purchased with the money saved by returning soda bottles, and then I'll take the trash out, understanding that he's had a long day and the last thing he needs is to hear me nagging. Finally, I will leap into bed, thanking God for another day as Wonder Woman!"

If we have tried that and failed, we think our only alternative is to quit! But when we take another trip back to the Garden of Eden, it is clear that God's dream for our lives has nothing to do with our performance. It has everything to do with our hearts. Fortunately, God doesn't quit believing in us even after we've stopped believing in ourselves. If God gave up on people who have failed, then Eve, Moses, Esther, David, Simon Peter, Mary Magdalene, and countless others would never have been used by him. In fact, God couldn't use anybody if he didn't use broken vessels.

Adam was formed from the dust outside the garden, but Eve was created from his side. As Martin Luther observed, God could have made Eve from Adam's toe to be lorded over or from his head to rule him, but he made her from his side to be his equal and companion. As a result of their sin, Adam and Eve were banished from that place of perfection and had to leave many of their dreams in the dust.

We, too, live in a fallen world where all our dreams do not come true. We know that. But I want to remind you . . . it's not over yet. There is a day coming! As the famous hymn "It Is Well" proclaims:

And Lord, haste the day when my faith shall be sight,
The clouds be rolled back as a scroll;
The trump shall resound, and the Lord shall descend,
Even so, it is well with my soul.[3]

HEAVEN ON EARTH

I don't know what you think of when you think of heaven. As a child, I used to think it would be very boring. I mean, how many rounds of "Kum Ba Ya" can you sing in the first million years?

I believe that when Jesus returns and establishes a new heaven and earth, we will all taste what it was like for Adam and Eve to walk with God in freedom. I believe that we will live the lives God always intended for us to live, but with no more sorrow. We will run like the wind.

Do you want to wait until you get to heaven, or do you want to join me now in celebrating God's love for us?

So here's my final question: Do you want to wait until you get to heaven, or do you want to join me now in celebrating God's love for us?

HOME AGAIN—AT LAST

I smiled to myself as I finished the last page of *The Wonderful Wizard of Oz*. Dorothy and her friends had found what they were looking for as they journeyed together, and now they were about to begin their new lives.

- The Scarecrow was returning to the Emerald City to be its mayor. They admired his wisdom.
- The Tin Woodsman would rule over the Winkies. They appreciated his heart.
- The Cowardly Lion was returning to the forest, where the animals had made him their king. They valued his courage.
- Dorothy was going home and carrying some of the color of Oz to a certain Aunt Em.

We are going home, too, but until we do, I want you to know that your Father is a King who treasures you as his princess. There is nothing that can change your position; it is your royal heritage. Nothing can happen to you today or tomorrow that is outside his care, so lift your head up and run like the wind!

Jesus has placed the stars within your reach.

Now to Him who is able to do exceedingly abundantly
above all that we ask or think, according to the power
that works in us, to Him be glory in the church by
Christ Jesus to all generations, forever and ever. Amen.
—Ephesians 3:20–21 NKJV

A Final Thought

SAVED BY LOVE

On a beautiful May morning, I drove with Mary Graham and Luci Swindoll to one of Dallas's oldest residential hotels. We had been invited to meet with Jenny Dyer and U2's Bono to hear the dream of the ONE Campaign. ONE is a new effort by Americans to rally Americans—ONE by ONE—to fight the emergency of global AIDS and extreme poverty. (When I wrote about Bono earlier on in this manuscript, I had no idea that God had already ordained that I would meet him just a few weeks later.)

As I stood side by side with Bono in a small, cramped elevator, I thought again that God's love has a way of leveling the ground beneath the cross. His love compels us to gather there and hear his heart.

Bono is an international rock star, but our conversation in the elevator that day was about our children and the fact that Bono's new shoes were killing his feet. Over coffee he began to talk to the six of us who were present about what really matters to him.

I have watched him perform many times, and I love his passion and energy, but it was never more evident than as he talked about God's heart for the poor.

I got up to refill my coffee, and as I looked out the window across the Dallas skyline, I suddenly became aware of God whispering to me. It was as if for just a moment he pulled back the curtain and gave me a glimpse of something I had never seen before. The only way I can express it in words is to say that it sounded like, *This is where you will find me.*

Let me try to illustrate what I mean.

A DIVINE MISSION

Imagine for a moment that you have been chosen to be a passenger on a space mission. You are thrilled and terrified at the same time. The day of the launch comes, and as you are strapped into your seat on the shuttle, you know that you are about to experience what few on this earth have ever experienced.

The launch goes without a hitch. Once you have gotten used to the curious feeling of being weightless (a gift to any woman!), you are captivated by the view of earth from space. Our huge planet seems so small. You can see the oceans and the shapes of the continents. It is breathtakingly beautiful.

This is not a routine mission but rather a divine mission. With new eyes you are able to focus in on different areas of the world. You turn first to a small town in mid-America. It's Sunday, and you can see families getting ready for church. You can hear the conversations that take place in the car or the kitchen. You watch a harried mother trying to get three children and a tuna casserole into the car on time. You listen in as a man and his wife argue over the appointment of a new pastor. You see a young girl look disgustedly at her reflection in the mirror and then reach for one more outfit to try on. You gaze through the stained-glass windows of a small church and watch as people fidget in the pews.

Pulling away from this scene, you focus in on a village in Africa. You can hear the cries of small children and feel the agony of a mother who holds a baby to a breast that is unable to produce enough milk to keep her child alive. The ground is dry, and the watering holes are small and polluted.

When you reflect for a moment, it seems as if one group is being destroyed by insignificant distractions while the other is being swept away by having their significance destroyed.

I have no heart to indulge in political speeches here, but I wonder if love wants to save us all? What if instead of turning our focus inward to what we perceive to be wrong with us, we turned it out to those who have been wronged? I have no doubt that if Jesus stepped into human flesh today, he would be with the poor. Yet the truth is that he is in human flesh, in you and in me.

We cling to the seventy or so years we have been promised and try to squeeze every ounce of happiness out of them. At best that is a disappointing pursuit, since what we really long for is to be home with our Father. What if, instead of trying to get the most out of this earthly life, we threw our lot in with him and got our feet as dirty as the road up to Golgotha?

We can all do something. Some of us can physically go to the poorest of the poor and hold them in our arms and recognize them for who they are: the image of God. We can all pray. We can all give something.

We can get involved with World Vision and lend our voices to the fight to end injustice (www.worldvision.org). Or we can join in with the ONE campaign and swell the ranks of those who want to end poverty one child at a time (www.ONE.org).

GOD'S AMAZING DREAM FOR YOUR LIFE

As I put the final words of this manuscript on paper today, I think of you and say a prayer for you. I pray that you know in the deepest place in your heart that you are loved. I pray that you understand that God never takes his eyes off you, that you are not alone. I pray that you will grasp hold of the truth that because you are God's daughter, his princess, anything is possible.

> *I believe with all my heart that God has a dream for your life that is far greater than any you could dream for yourself.*

I believe with all my heart that God has a dream for your life that is far greater than any you could dream for yourself. When God looks at you, he sees a woman whom he passionately loves. That love compelled him to give his Son to redeem you from the nightmare of a life spent apart from him. No matter whether any of your smaller dreams are realized on this earth, God has an amazing dream for your life that nothing and no one can touch.

God's dream for you outweighs every other dream in your life. One day, you will at last stand before the Lamb of God. By his grace and mercy, you will hear him say, "Well done, good and faithful servant; you were faithful over a few things, I will make you ruler over many things. Enter into the joy of your lord" (Matthew 25:21 NKJV).

Notes

A Letter from Sheila
1. Henry Cloud, *Changes That Heal: How to Understand the Past to Ensure a Healthier Future* (Grand Rapids: Zondervan, 1997).

Introduction: *Aunt Em, Dorothy, and Mrs. Pirie*
1. L. Frank Baum, *The Wonderful Wizard of Oz* (New York: HarperTrophy, 2001), 12.

Chapter 1: *Somewhere Over the Rainbow*—What Is Freedom?
1. "Deep in the Heart of Texas" words by June Hershey and music by Don Swander © 1941 Melody Lane Publication. Copyright renewed. International Copyright Secured. Used by Permission. All rights reserved.

Chapter 3: *If I Only Had a Heart!*—Free to Love and Be Loved
1. Baum, *The Wonderful Wizard of Oz* (New York: HarperTrophy, 2001), 73.
2. "The Love of God," Frederick M. Lehman ©1917.

Chapter 5: *The Ruby Slippers*—Free to Receive the Desires of My Heart
1. Joel Chandler Harris, *The Classic Tales of Brer Rabbit* (Philadelphia: Running Press, 2004), 49. Used by permission.
2. Bruce Wilkinson, *The Prayer of Jabez: Breaking Through to the Blessed Life* (Sisters, OR: Multnomah, 2000).
3. C. S. Lewis, *Mere Christianity* (San Francisco: HarperSanFrancisco, 2001), 226. All rights reserved. Used by permission of C.S. Lewis Company.

Chapter 7: *The Cowardly Lion*—Free to Let Go of Shame
1. *Pretty Woman* © 1990. Buena Vista Home Entertainment / Touchstone.
2. *Educating Rita* © 1983. Sony Pictures.

Chapter 11: *A Very Bad Wizard*—Changed by Disappointment
1. Baum, *The Wonderful Wizard of Oz* (New York: HarperTrophy, 2001), 174.
2. Sheila Walsh, *I'm Not Wonder Woman, but God Made Me Wonderful* (Nashville: Thomas Nelson, 2006).

Chapter 12: *The Scarecrow's Gift*—Changed By the Love of God
1. "Beneath the Cross of Jesus" lyrics by Elizabeth C. Clephane, music by Frederick C. Maker ©1868.
2. Ibid.
3. Ibid.
4. Ibid.
5. Ibid.

Chapter 13: *We're Off to See the Wizard!*—Changed by the Journey
1. Kate DiCamillo, *The Miraculous Journey of Edward Tulane* (Cambridge, MA: Candlewick, 2006).
2. Excerpt from "Little Gidding" in *Four Quartets*, copyright 1942 by T.S. Eliot and renewed by Esme Valerie Eliot, reprinted by permission of Harcourt, Inc.
3. Max Lucado, *The Cure for the Common Life* (Nashville: W Publishing, a division of Thomas Nelson, Inc., 2006). All rights reserved.

Chapter 15: *Suddenly, the Wind Changed*—Dreaming at the Crossroads
1. "Who Am I" by Mark Hall. © Word Music Group. (Admin. by EMI Club Zoo Music). All rights reserved.
2. John Milton, *Paradise Lost*, Book IX, lines 780–84.

Chapter 16: *You've Had the Power All Along*—Dreaming with Our Father
1. *Chariots of Fire* ©1981. Enigma Productions, Goldcrest Film Ltd., Warner Bros.
2. Taken from *Lost Women of the Bible* by Carolyn Custis James. Copyright © 2005 by Carolyn Custis James. Used by permission of Zondervan.
3. "It is Well With My Soul" words by Horatio G. Spafford, music by Philip P. Bliss © 1873.

THE CAMPAIGN TO MAKE
POVERTY HISTORY
WWW.ONE.ORG

There is a plague of biblical proportions taking place in Africa right now, but we can beat this crisis, if we each do our part. Step ONE is signing the ONE petition, to join the ONE Campaign.

The ONE Campaign is a new effort to rally Americans—ONE by ONE—to fight global AIDS and extreme poverty. We are engaging Americans everywhere we gather—in churches and synagogues, on the internet and college campuses, at community meetings and concerts. To learn more about The ONE Campaign, go to www.one.org and sign the online petition.

ONE Voice can make a difference.
Let God work through you; join the ONE Campaign now!

This campaign is brought to you by